Sweepstakes,
Prize Promotions,
Games
and
Contests

Sweepstakes, Prize Promotions, Games and Contests

Jeffrey P. Feinman
Robert D. Blashek
Richard J. McCabe

DOW JONES-IRWIN
Homewood, Illinois 60430

ISBN 0-87094-643-9

Library of Congress Catalog Card No. 86-70515

Printed in the United States of America

1 2 3 4 5 6 7 8 9 0 MP 3 2 1 0 9 8 7 6

DEDICATION

*To Ron, Ted, Murray, and Bobbe,
the best practitioners of the art
and science of prize promotions.*

PREFACE

This book is for anyone who has a product or service to sell. It is essentially for marketing people, but it will be useful for the businessperson who wants to increase sales, build traffic, gain market share, or establish a position of leadership.

Basically, the whole concept of promotion is to offer something that consumers do not expect in the normal course of doing business. But the narrower topic of prize promotion adds the element of gratification to the unexpected. It presents the consumer with an opportunity to win a valuable prize for performing some particular process—visiting a store to fill out an entry blank, buying a product, or trying a service. Prize offers are based on a basic principle of psychology—positive reinforcement—in which the subject experiences a certain pleasurable consequence following the performance of a specific task.

Prize promotion is probably the fastest growing area of marketing. Just 25 years ago people were predicting the demise of the prize promotion industry. These Cassandras were obviously mistaken, since with every passing year we are seeing a dramatic increase, not only in the *number* of promotions, but in the various *types* and *users* of promotions. The major reason for this phenomenon is most likely due to the fact that products and marketing have gone through several stages in their development.

In the first stage, before the turn of the century, a product was sold simply on its superiority. An individual was capable of making a superb wooden bowl or a magnificent horseshoe, or individuals were known far and wide for their unique sewing skills, and so the sale of a product was based on its quality or perceived quality.

With the Industrial Revolution it became possible for mass manufacturers to create products of equal quality. A good organic chemist with $200 could figure out the formula for any of the various medicines or cleaning products. Anyone who had the financial resources to invest in machinery was capable of producing a competitive product. Therefore, product superiority diminished. Except for products that were protected by patents, the age of product superiority was over.

In the second stage in the development of marketing, marketers began to ask, "How do we differentiate our product from all the others on the shelves that are of equal quality? How can we cut it in the marketplace?" The answer was ADVERTISING superiority. The manufacturer used advertising to create a unique position for his product. Companies turned to advertising as a response to parity products. If all products were essentially the same, then the secret was to make them *appear* different in the mind of the consumer. Fab and Tide were chemically the same, but the creative imagination of the advertising community could instill a difference in the consumer's mind. Although Camel, Lucky Strike, and Old Gold were essentially the same tobacco product, creative advertising convinced the consumer that there were wide differences between them. Consumers were essentially buying advertising, not products.

By the 1960s, when most advertising seemed to be taking on similar characteristics, we were entering stage three. We were fast approaching parity advertising. Many advertisers had found new and exciting ways to extoll the virtues of their products. Then, all of a sudden, there was a formula for good advertisements, and everyone knew the elements that a successful ad must contain. If you had examined ads for a dozen different dog foods, you would have seen a striking similarity among them—dogs running and jumping, their tails wagging as they raced to the bowl of dog food. It became apparent that just as there were few unique products, there were few unique advertising campaigns.

A recent issue of *TV Guide* contained 11 pages of cigarette ads, and they all depicted the same thing—a good-looking man in the great outdoors or at a posh party enjoying a cigarette. So now, in this third stage in the development of product marketing, we have advertising clutter. As each of the marketing disciplines evolved, they all reached a clutter level. Regardless of how good your product may be, there are probably many others just as worthy. All are attractively packaged. All are attractively and expensively advertised.

Now that we have product parity *and* advertising parity, what's next? How do you create a demonstrable difference for your product? With PROMOTION superiority—prize promotion in particular. What Ventura Associates has consistently demonstrated is that prize promotion is capable of differentiating products *and* advertising by giving the consumer "something extra." So when people go to the supermarket and see endless rolls of paper towels each one screaming "New, Blue, and Improved!"—it is the one that says "WIN $25,000! Free Game Ticket Inside" that catches their attention.

In the first call I made in this business, nearly 20 years ago, I asked the client why he was running a sweepstakes, and he said that he had a full-page ad in *TV Guide* and didn't know what to do with it. Today, no client would use a contest simply as a filler for an ad; he would use it to accomplish a specific objective, whether it's traffic building, coupon redemption, or generating consumer involvement. Prize promotions were once the exclusive province of the packaged goods and food market industries. Today, anyone can effectively apply the chance to win a valuable prize—the chance to win a dream—to his business. Prize promotion can be the solution to almost any business problem that requires a specific consumer action. Fund raisers use sweepstakes, and so do airlines, soft drink bottlers, newspapers, and broadcasters. In fact, there is hardly a business you can think of that has not used prize promotions successfully.

Prize promotions are so ubiquitous today that there will be a dozen or so a month. Then why, with identical budgets, do some prize promotions succeed and others fail? Why do some draw millions of entries and others a mere trickle? Why do some accomplish their marketing goals and others fall short of the mark? As in most fields of endeavor, the person with the most experience in a variety of situations will be the most effective. The reason I decided to write this book is that I have designed and administered thousands of prize promotions and have developed some unique skills in making them work for advertisers.

My background in this field is actually related to a case of arrested development—I never stopped saving popsicle wrappers! When I was going to college I planned to go into the advertising business. When I graduated, people were surprised to hear that I was going into sales promotion because it had always been considered a job that people took when they couldn't get into advertising. But I actively sought out the opportunity to work with a promotional firm. It seemed to me that advertising, despite its obvious creative aspects, was a passive medium. I wanted to work in an area where the fruits of my labor were tangible and immediate.

Fifteen years ago, I started my own sales promotion firm, Ventura Associates. Today it is one of the leading prize promotion companies in the country. Ventura designs and implements thousands of contests and sweepstakes for companies including Revlon, American Express, General Foods, NBC, and hundreds of Fortune 500 companies. In addition, we handle prize offers for fund-raising organizations, industrial companies, and direct mailers of every product imaginable.

In this book I hope to pass on some of the information Bob Blashek, Rick McCabe, and I have acquired and techniques we have developed over the years. It should be valuable to anyone who is considering using a prize promotion or to the prize promoter who wants to make his sweepstakes more effective.

ACKNOWLEDGMENTS

This book was made a reality by Robin Ellen Hanna, whose skills and dedication are nothing short of extraordinary. Also, special kudos to Allen Fay, M.D., for his inspiration and input.

In addition, the authors wish to thank the staff of Ventura Associates for their readings and re-readings and re-readings again, and Ken and Mary Mobert for their insights and participation.

Jeffrey Feinman

CONTENTS

CHAPTER ONE

The History of Prize Promotion

It was P. T. Barnum, appropriately, who conducted the first recorded contest in the United States. In 1850, he offered a $200 prize for a song, "Ode to America," written to promote "The Swedish Nightingale," Jenny Lind. In 1897, Eastman Kodak held a photography contest to increase public interest in picture-taking. But to trace the evolution of lotteries and, later, prize promotions, we have to go back to biblical times.

"LOT"—IT'S ORIGINAL DEFINITION AND DERIVATION

The word *lot* originated from the Teutonic root *hleut.* It was used to describe an object, such as a disk, pebble, or bean, which was either cast or drawn to make some sort of decision (often in disputes over division of land or goods). It was believed that these decisions were made under Divine Guidance.

In English, the word *hlot* or *hlodd* evolved into *lot* in the 13th century. In Dutch, it was *lot;* in Danish, *lod;* in Swedish, *lott;* and in Icelandic, *hlautr.* The Romance languages adopted the teutonic word, and it became *lot* in French, *lote* in Portuguese, *loto* in Spanish, and *lotto* in Italian. Scholars differ on how the English word *lottery* was derived. Some believe it came from the Italian *lotteria,* while others say it came from Flanders' *lotterie.*

THE BIBLE

Whatever its derivation, evidence of lotteries is found as early as Old Testament times. The use of the lot is reported throughout the Bible. Lots were used to decide everything from the division of land to political and labor issues.

The instances of lots described in the Bible are staggering in number and type. The first King of Israel was chosen by lot. Lev. 16:8 states: "And Aaron shall cast lots upon the two goats; one lot for the Lord, and the other lot for the scapegoat." In the book of Numbers we find that allocation of land was determined by chance. It is written there that, after taking a census of the Israelites, Moses apportioned the land west of the Jordan "for inheritance according to the number of names to each tribe" (Num.

26:55). In order to avoid jealousy, the territories were divided by lot.

Distribution of unpleasant duties were also decided by lot. In Jon. 1:6, ancient sailors frightened by the tempest cast lots to choose the party that would sail, and "The lot fell upon Jonah." Legal controversies were also settled by lot. "The lot causeth contentions to cease and parteth between the mighty" (Josh. 7:16). Lots were also recommended by Solomon as a method of settling disputes.

THE NEW TESTAMENT

The proliferation of the use of lots continues in the New Testament. Divine will was ascertained by the casting of lots. Stones of different colors or inscribed with symbols were put into a vessel that was then shaken until one of the stones popped out. People believed that this method of selection removed any human element and that the choice was made by God. After the death of Judas Iscariot, the casting of lots was used to choose his successor as an apostle—either Joseph or Matthias. "And they prayed and said, 'Lord . . . show which one of these two Thou has chosen to take the place in this ministry . . .,' And they cast lots . . . and the lot fell on Matthias" (Acts 1:24).

THE ROMANS

The Romans continued the use of lotteries as a method of predicting events. Sortes—rods or plates bearing inscriptions—were drawn. The interpretation of the inscription provided answers to questions on a wide variety of subjects. A forerunner of present-day lotteries, the questioner paid an oracle to draw the sortes. Cicero (106–43 B.C.) renounced these drawings saying, "The whole scheme of divination by lots was fraudulently contrived from mercenary motives or as a means of encouraging superstition and error."

At the lavish banquets of the day, the Roman emperors distributed gifts to their guests using lots to determine who would get what. Elagabulus distributed chances inscribed on spoons at his feasts and games. The inscriptions determined the utility and value of the gift that would go to the bearer of that spoon. A guest might receive something as valuable as 10 pounds of gold or 10 camels, or as useless as 10 flies!

Augustus gave his followers gifts by selling them lots. The articles represented by these lots were a mystery in addition to being of unequal value. Everyone was required to buy a lot and run the risk of loss or gain. This proceeding, with equal payments and unequal prizes or no prize at all, parallels the lotteries in Europe and North America in the 17th and 18th centuries.

There is evidence that the first lottery used to sell goods took place in Rome. Italian merchants were said to keep an "Urn of Fortune" from which their customers were permitted to draw a ticket inscribed with the names of various articles. The customers then drew another ticket inscribed with a price. The holder of the ticket was thus entitled to the merchandise inscribed on the first ticket at the price stated on the second.

THE GREEKS

In other references of this period, the *Iliad* notes that Greek heroes marked their own lots and cast them to determine who would have the honor of fighting Hector. In the first century, Tacitus records that the Teutonic tribes practiced divination and wizardry using lots to decide whether a battle should be fought, and to determine the leaders and the fate of prisoners. The drawing of lots was also used to determine the answers to questions such as: Who shall be sacrificed for food? Who will do battle? and Who is guilty of a crime? The answers to such questions, as well as anything determined by lot, were not subject to argument. The decision was final.

MEDIEVAL PERIOD

In the medieval period—from 1443 to 1449—there is evidence of lotteries in places such as Oudenarde, Utrecht, Ghent, Bruges, and L'Ecluse, where the earliest recorded lottery of this period took place. Its purpose was to raise 10,000 salut d'or for construction of walls and fortifications.

In 1446, English and Scottish names were found among those of participants in Brugeouis lotteries. This is particularly interesting because it shows that over a century before lotteries appeared in Britain, chances were known to Englishmen.

In the first half of the 16th century, there are records of numerous lotteries held in territories now known as Holland, Belgium, and France. In 1526, an edict was handed down forbidding all unlicensed lotteries, with a penalty of confiscation of prizes and all money received. This is probably an early step in the evolution of state lotteries.

ENGLAND

Although the earliest record of an English lottery was the one held by Queen Elizabeth in 1568, historians believe that lotteries took place earlier. An example may be a lottery chartered in 1566 to raise funds to repair harbors. However, lotteries were not used extensively in England until the 17th century when many private lotteries were held for the benefit of both individuals and corporations. These personal enterprises continued until the end of the 17th century when they became a public nuisance; they were suppressed in 1699. The suppression of these private ventures paved the way for all kinds of state lotteries, which continued for about 130 years until they were abolished in 1826.

While important public works were funded with lotteries, abuses in the system, such as gambling on chances, are to blame for lotteries' fall from grace. Despite this, many lotteries (under names like art unions, sweepstakes, subscription funds, ballots, and tombolas) were held with or without official sanction.

EARLIEST LOTTERIES HELD ELSEWHERE

In 1470, in Augsburg in the ancient duchy of Bavaria, a lottery was held that sold 36,000 tickets. While there is evidence of lotteries held at L'Ecluse and Lille in the 15th century, the lottery was formally introduced to France in 1533 by the Italians. These lotteries were known as blanques (in Italian, bianca) simply because white tickets outnumbered black tickets. In 1659, at the time of the marriage of Louis XIV, French state lotteries were organized. These continue today as an aid to France's financial resources.

In Italy, the earliest documented lottery took place in Florence in 1530. A new kind of lottery was introduced by a Genoese senate member in 1623 and was known as the famous "groco del lotto."

NORTH AMERICA

The Virginia Lotteries of 1611 are the first known lotteries in North America. Experiencing difficulty in supporting its settlement in Jamestown, the Virginia Company of London petitioned the king for relief. This merchant group was granted a charter in 1612 to conduct one or more lotteries in England within a year's time. Continued permission after that year was at the discretion of the king.

In an early use of advertising, a ballad was written to stir up enthusiasm for the lottery. "London's Lotterie" was sung to the tune of "Lusty Gallant" and proclaimed the need for colonization of the future United States. It appealed to both patriotism and religion, all the while stressing the value of the prizes!

In 1619, complaints began to surface that the lottery had demoralized business and industry. A year later, with little warning, the Privy Council halted the lotteries. Another reason for the ban was discord among officers of the Virginia Company itself, with accusations that money was misappropriated. Whatever the reasons, the ban was a tremendous blow for the Virginia Company and its struggling colony in America.

In the American colonies, lotteries soon became a part of everyday life. Many reasons account for the lottery's acceptance in the newly formed America: the prevalence and popularity of lotteries in the Old World, economic pressures associated with establishment of governments and cities, and a general lack of moral opposition to lotteries. All of these reasons stimulated the already recognized and accepted gambling instinct.

In America, as in England, lotteries fell into two categories: drawings by individuals for personal profit and drawings legally sanctioned for public benefit. The official attitude toward lotteries proceeded through four stages:

1. Laissez-faire.
2. Legal sanctions for some drawings and no restrictions on others.
3. Outlawing unauthorized lotteries.
4. Total prohibition.

Lotteries were often used to dispose of household goods or land because it was an assured way of getting a fair price. Even Thomas Jefferson wrote approvingly of lotteries used for these purposes. For the most part, such lotteries were conducted with the public interest in mind. The funds raised were used to build bridges, churches, schools, and roads. As a matter of fact, one of the most famous lotteries of the time, in Pennsylvania, raised money for the "College, Academy and Charitable School of Philadelphia," now known as the University of Pennsylvania.

As could have been expected, when lotteries became popular, their sponsors and promoters were often found to be acting in bad faith. Corrupt promoters sometimes fixed lotteries so that tickets for the most valuable prizes were never drawn, or they used inferior merchandise for the majority of the prizes. It was not unusual for a promoter to disappear with the proceeds without even holding his drawing.

Merchants of the day opposed lotteries because they saw them as competition. Money used to purchase lottery tickets might otherwise have been used to buy goods or services. But for the most part, the public was indifferent. The Society of Friends was the only group to consistently oppose lotteries. The Quakers' disapproval of all types of gambling, and many forms of amusement in general, accounts for their opposition. However, at that time the Quakers were not a large group and their opinion had little effect on lotteries.

Nonetheless, lotteries were eventually widely banned. As cited by governments of the day, the main reason for banning unlicensed lotteries was because of the effect they had on the poor. Apparently all forms of gambling had a particular appeal to the lower classes.

Eventually, local governments considered regulating lotteries rather than banning them altogether. New York, Massachusetts, Connecticut, Rhode Island, and Pennsylvania were among the first states to prohibit lotteries that didn't have legislative approval. Virginia's legislation came much later than the other colonies. The reason for Virginia's tolerance was perhaps due to the fact that several eminent figures were often associated with lotteries—George Washington, to name one.

Why were lotteries licensed rather than abolished altogether? The main reason seems to be that the people wanted these drawings. They believed they could be conducted honestly and felt it was an individual's business how he risked his money. Also, there was a high degree of financial instability in the provinces at the time. Funds were needed to finance wars with the French and the Indians. There was also an unfavorable balance of trade with England. Lotteries were viewed as a viable solution to all these problems.

There was a set method for operation of lotteries in early America:

1. A group or individual would petition the General Assembly to obtain permission to conduct a lottery.
2. After authorizing the lottery, the legislature would give the group a set of rules to follow for the operation of the lottery.
3. Appointments of directors and managers were made.
4. Managers were bonded to protect against fraud.
5. Numbered lottery tickets were produced in triplicate: one for the purchaser (signed by the seller), one sealed in a box, and the third kept in a ticket book used for comparison if a mistake occurred or fraud were suspected.
6. The drawing took place in a public room conducted by the managers. The sealed box containing the tickets was opened, the contents were mixed, and a person unconnected with the lottery drew the winning tickets.
7. A drawing was made from a second box containing tickets imprinted with a description of a prize and others that were blank. If the second ticket drawn was imprinted, then the holder of the numbered ticket was a winner.

Many schools of the day sought the use of lotteries for funding. King's College in New York, today known as Columbia University, was the first college granted a license to raise funds by lottery. The first lottery of any kind to be approved by the Connecticut Assembly was for the benefit of Yale. In an unusual example, the College of New Jersey, now Princeton University, was refused the right to hold a lottery by the New Jersey legislators. The college then petitioned Connecticut for a license to hold the lottery in that state. In 1753, the Connecticut Assembly granted the license; the drawing was held in Stamford and raised 7,500 pounds. Princeton was not permitted to hold a lottery in New Jersey until 1762, nearly 10 years later.

Harvard College was not as successful in its use of a lottery. The college received legislative approval in 1765, but the financial situation in Massachusetts was in great turmoil and residents had little money to spend on lotteries.

At about the same time, as early as 1761, the British government was not favorably disposed to colonial lotteries. In 1769, a letter was sent to the governors of Delaware, Georgia, Massachusetts, New Hampshire, New Jersey, New York, North Carolina, Pennsylvania, South Carolina, and West Florida that in essence directed them not to authorize any lottery without the express permission of the crown. So, for a number of years after this edict was handed down, the only colonies that conducted lotteries were Rhode Island, Maryland, and Connecticut.

After 1789, lotteries reached their greatest period of popularity. In the late 1700s, America experienced enormous growth, which in turn led to increasing demands from American citizens. There were roads, canals, and bridges to be built, and sewage and transportation systems to be developed. By this time lotteries were a strong part of the country's economy; they were a proven method of raising funds to meet all these new demands. All was well with the lottery system, but it would not last for long.

As the lotteries increased, there was a growing need for lottery contractors and ticket brokers. The people who assumed these functions were those who recognized the tremendous opportunities the lottery system offered. These people often exploited this system for personal gain.

Ticket brokers of the day relieved lottery managers of the task of selling tickets. They usually purchased large numbers of tickets at a discount and then sold them at their original price. Eventually, the tickets were sold exclusively at the broker's place of business, usually in shops and in branches across the country.

For a fee, lottery contractors assumed control of the entire operation of a lottery including the drawing. Contractors used brokers as outlets for the sale of lottery tickets. This led to the birth of big business. Business concerns of all types used the successful techniques developed by lottery contractors and profited greatly from them. In fact, the lottery gave rise to private banking and later to stock brokerages. Some of this country's largest banking institutions were founded by lottery contractors and brokers. The First National Bank of New York City, chartered in 1863 and now known as Citibank, and the Chase National Bank, chartered in 1873, were both founded by John Thompson, a former lottery broker.

"Insurance," a practice used widely by the middle of the 19th century, was meant to aid individuals who couldn't afford the price of a lottery ticket. This practice became one of the most lucrative parts of a ticket agent's business and subsequently the subject of severe criticism. The "insurance" business required the new practice of extending a drawing over a period of several weeks. A fixed number of tickets were drawn each day, and, as time passed, people began to speculate as to when undrawn numbers would be chosen. Ticket brokers took advantage of this speculation by accepting bets on which numbers would be selected the following day. Newspapers printed the "insurance rates," or odds, on a daily basis. Smart lottery players soon found that they could not lose if they took part in the insurance scheme. For example, an individual holding a lottery ticket that was yet undrawn could bet that his ticket was one of the many blank ones sold. When the ticket was drawn and turned out to be a prize winning ticket, he of course received the prize on the ticket. But even if the ticket were a blank, the holder was a winner because he had "insured" his investment in the lottery ticket.

As might be expected, "insurance" practices led to many abuses of the lottery system. It did not take long for the governments of various states to take remedial action. By 1840, 12 states had antilottery legislation, while over the next 20 years additional states, including Maryland, Alabama, and New Jersey, outlawed lotteries altogether.

Meanwhile, the Louisiana lottery came through this rough period of regulation virtually unscathed. All through the 1880s, the Louisiana lottery was subjected to challenges by the courts and the legislature, and yet it somehow survived this onslaught. The staying power of this lottery led to accusations that legislators accepted bribes to vote in favor of individual lottery schemes.

The unsavory situation in Louisiana was not typical of other states. In 1878 antilottery bills began to be introduced in Congress. Eventually, even Louisiana was the victim of this rampant opposition to lotteries.

President Harrison was one of the first public figures of this time to express the sentiment of the public when he denounced lotteries, saying that they "debauched and defrauded" the people of the United States. In 1890, he asked Congress for severe legislation that would curb lotteries. Two years later, Congress passed a bill that prohibited the use of the mails for the purposes of a lottery. It is not surprising that this bill made it through Congress since all but 2 of the 44 states had already banned lottery activity in whole or in part. Aside from the rampant exploitation of privately sponsored lotteries, a major reason behind the antilottery legislation was the potential use of lotteries to produce revenue for the government. Thus, we witness the birth of the state-run lottery.

The antilottery laws of the 1930s and 40s limited the use of chance in prize promotions conducted by marketers of that era. Therefore, the contest of skill, which eliminated chance, became the most prevalent type of prize promotion. After a time, state legislators began to realize that sweepstakes and other types of prize promotions were not being run like lotteries or any form of gambling, and restrictions on their use were relaxed.

In the 1960s many forms of prize promotion grew increasingly popular. However, this burgeoning popularity came to an abrupt halt after investigations held in 1968 by the Federal Trade Commission and Congress revealed abuses within the prize promotion industry. It wasn't until the late 1970s that prize promotion regained its former stature in the marketing industry. With the advent of state lotteries, legislation governing prize promotion cleared the way for a resurgence of its former popularity. It is estimated that the number of nationally advertised prize promotions has more than tripled since 1975, and today, contests, sweepstakes, and games are used by every kind of business, with entrants including everyone from homemakers, children, and senior citizens to executives and professionals—people in every walk of life and in every age and income group.

CHAPTER TWO

The Types of Prize Promotions

When referring to prize promotions, consumers and businesspeople mistakenly use the terms *lottery, drawing, raffle, contest, competition, sweepstakes, game,* and *puzzle* interchangeably. Here we will define these terms and show you how they differ. In later chapters, we discuss how each of these devices can be used to attain specific goals.

Actually, all that these terms have in common is that they are classed under the general heading of prize offers and, with the exception of contests, they all contain an element of chance.

Chapter Three outlines the legal aspects of a lottery. You will see that, for the marketer's purposes at present, a lottery has no place in business. Therefore, in this chapter we will concern ourselves with the broad types of prize promotions that can work for your business.

SWEEPSTAKES

Sweepstakes are also known as drawings, raffles, chances, or competitions. In this type of offer, the key element is the completion of an entry form giving the consumer an opportunity to win a prize through some form of random drawing.

There are essentially three major kinds of sweepstakes:

1. Random Drawing Sweepstakes. In this kind of offer we can request, but not require, a box top or some other proof of purchase. We simply ask the consumer to complete an entry blank and mail it to sweepstakes headquarters or drop it off at a specified store. The winners are then selected in a random drawing (see Illustration 1).

2. Lucky Number Sweepstakes. In lucky number sweepstakes, the winning number is predetermined at random. The consumer is given a game ticket with a lucky number on it. He or she then visits a specified retail store and compares the lucky number against the winning number on the store's display. If the number matches, he or she is a winner (see Illustration 2). Lucky number sweepstakes are also successful in direct mail offers. In this case, the consumer mails in the entry form, and an independent judging organization screens the lucky numbers against the winning numbers that have been selected.

ILLUSTRATION 1 I Have a Winner-Takes-All Sweepstakes for You!, Theragran

A conventional random drawing sweepstakes. Because the entry form is in the ad, complete rules must also be included.

Courtesy of E. R. Squibb & Sons, Inc.

ILLUSTRATION 2 Customer Entry Verification Form, Great American Magazines

Consecutive numbering and/or jet imaging can give everyone an exclusive number. Winning numbers are selected, and all numbers submitted are screened against the winning numbers list. A second chance drawing is held to award all unclaimed prizes.

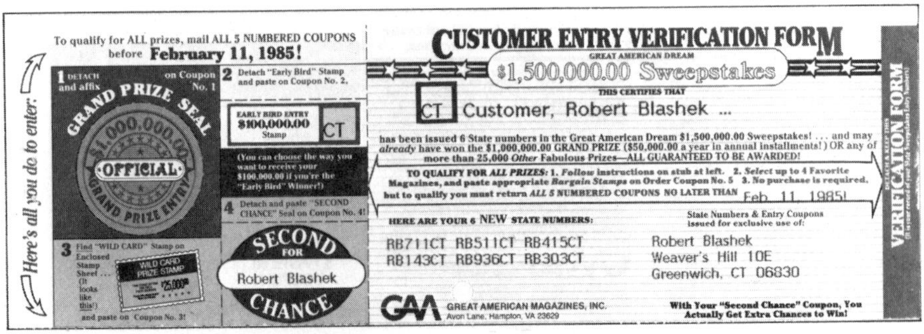

Courtesy of Great American Magazines.

In a lucky number offer, we simply sequentially number coupons, free-standing inserts, magazine pop-up cards, or game cards. So, if we distributed 5 million pieces, they would be numbered from 1 to 5,000,000. Then we randomly select the winning number. For example, if there were 5 million free-standing inserts and we randomly selected 5,108 as the winning number, one piece would have that winning number and the remaining 4,999,999 would not. The inserts would then be distributed, and consumers would be advised to come to the store and compare their numbers with the display that would read: "5,108 Is the Winning Number."

ILLUSTRATION 3 Sandwich Days Sweepstakes (with coupon)

A sweepstakes overlay will dramatically increase coupon redemption.

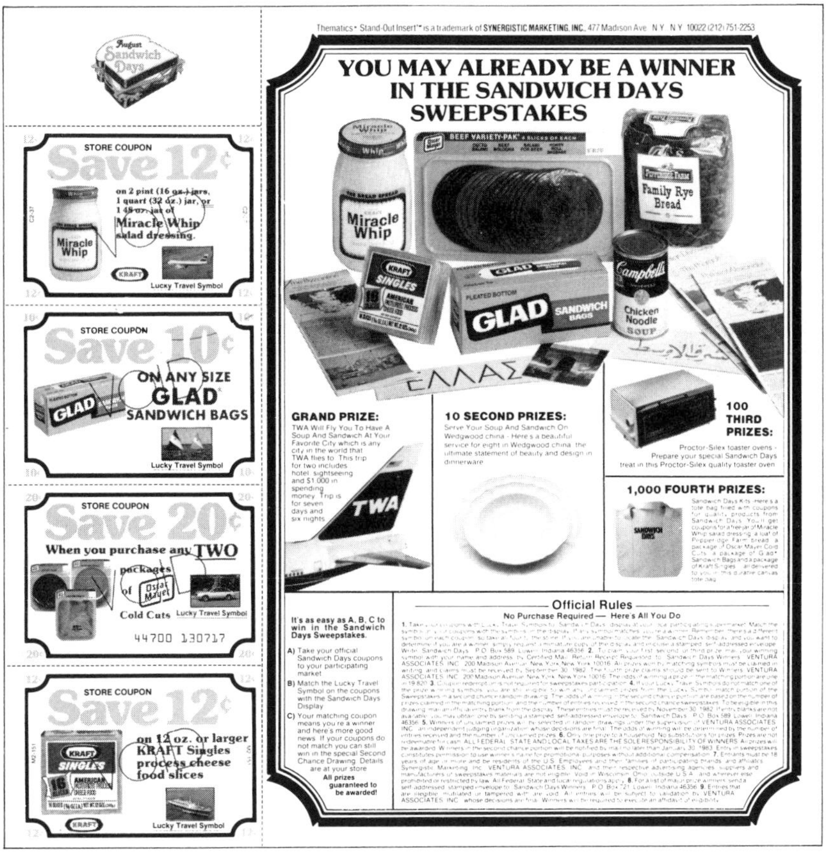

Courtesy of Kraft.

The recent trend in lucky numbers offers is to require consumers to match a lucky symbol, like a star or a flag, rather than a number. The mechanics of lucky number and lucky symbol sweepstakes are the same. In the case of a lucky symbol offer, we might produce a million coupons with a losing symbol, say, for example, a plum, and a coupon with a winning symbol, a cherry. We would randomly drop the winning piece into the entire distribution, and the consumer who matches the symbol on their coupon with that on a display or product package is the winner (see Illustration 3).

Lucky number and lucky symbol sweepstakes have given rise to second chance drawings where, if the lucky symbol or lucky number is not matched and the prize is not claimed, consumers are then invited to send in an entry form, and a winner is selected by random drawing. This assures that the prize or prizes will actually be awarded.

3. Games. A game is nothing more than a sweepstakes with the following added benefits: continuity, involvement, and instant gratification. The mechanics of a game offer involves the distribution of the game pieces with a controlled number of winning symbols. It offers the consumer the opportunity to come in, rub off a card, and instantly know if he or she is the winner. The use of a variety of production techniques, such as a rub-off, a wash-off, or a perforated seal, allows for instant gratification.

Instant gratification plus so-called playability—the ability to get a game card, rub off a spot, and instantly see the winning or losing symbol—have brought game offers to prominence in the fast-food, supermarket, and gasoline station businesses (see Illustration 4).

The three kinds of sweepstakes we have discussed are used by sponsors who distribute merchandise through traditional channels, such as retail outlets or restaurants. However, sweepstakes are also frequently used by direct mailers, and all the same techniques apply. Direct mailers generally use lucky number sweepstakes because it gives them the opportunity to use the key copy line: "You May Have Already Won One Million Dollars!" The use of computer techniques allows direct mailers to go one step further and personalize the piece. An example of this is shown in Illustration 5.

CONTESTS OF SKILL

In a contest of skill the key operating element is, not surprisingly, skill. This may mean challenging the consumer to write in 25 words or less why he or she likes a product or having the consumer complete a rhyme or solve a puzzle. The winner is selected based solely on the entrant's use of a special talent or skill appropriate to the particular contest.

ILLUSTRATION 4 Great Gull Rabbit Hunt Game Cards (not scratched off; scratched off)

Games often offer three chances to win: match symbols for instant win; collect letters to spell a word and win; and enter nonwinning game piece in the sweepstakes drawing.

Courtesy of Gull Gas.

For many years, the contest of skill was the standard prize promotion technique. However, liberalization of laws in the early 1960s permitted sweepstakes in most every state, and this diminished the popularity of contests because of their severe limitations compared with sweepstakes. The limitations are:

1. Participation in a contest of skill requires time, effort, energy, and sometimes even talent. Obviously, since en-

ILLUSTRATION 5 American Family Publishers Letter: "J. W. Feinman, You May Have Just Won Ten Million Dollars"

Computerization personalizes the message and helps to get the consumer involved with the offer.

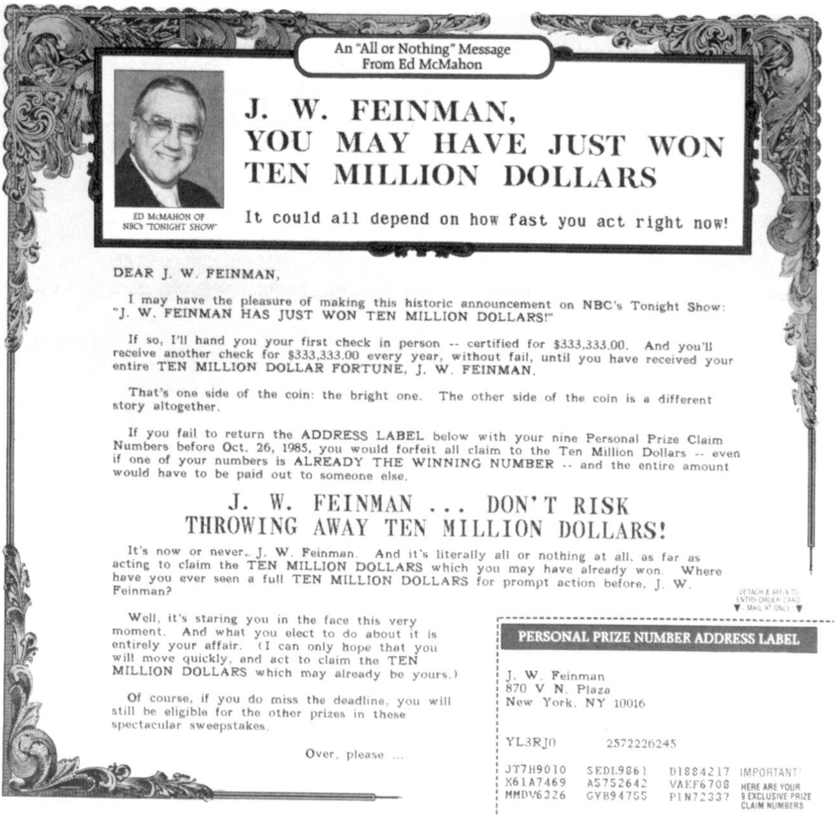
An "All or Nothing" Message
From Ed McMahon

ED McMAHON OF NBC's "TONIGHT SHOW"

J. W. FEINMAN,
YOU MAY HAVE JUST WON
TEN MILLION DOLLARS

It could all depend on how fast you act right now!

DEAR J. W. FEINMAN,

I may have the pleasure of making this historic announcement on NBC's Tonight Show: "J. W. FEINMAN HAS JUST WON TEN MILLION DOLLARS!"

If so, I'll hand you your first check in person -- certified for $333,333.00. And you'll receive another check for $333,333.00 every year, without fail, until you have received your entire TEN MILLION DOLLAR FORTUNE, J. W. FEINMAN.

That's one side of the coin: the bright one. The other side of the coin is a different story altogether.

If you fail to return the ADDRESS LABEL below with your nine Personal Prize Claim Numbers before Oct. 26, 1985, you would forfeit all claim to the Ten Million Dollars -- even if one of your numbers is ALREADY THE WINNING NUMBER -- and the entire amount would have to be paid out to someone else.

J. W. FEINMAN ... DON'T RISK
THROWING AWAY TEN MILLION DOLLARS!

It's now or never, J. W. Feinman. And it's literally all or nothing at all, as far as acting to claim the TEN MILLION DOLLARS which you may have already won. Where have you ever seen a full TEN MILLION DOLLARS for prompt action before, J. W. Feinman?

Well, it's staring you in the face this very moment. And what you elect to do about it is entirely your affair. (I can only hope that you will move quickly, and act to claim the TEN MILLION DOLLARS which may already be yours.)

Of course, if you do miss the deadline, you will still be eligible for the other prizes in these spectacular sweepstakes.

Over, please ...

DETACH & AFFIX TO ENTRY-ORDER CARD — MAIL AT ONCE!

PERSONAL PRIZE NUMBER ADDRESS LABEL

J. W. Feinman
870 V N. Plaza
New York, NY 10016

YL3RJ0 2572226245

JT7H9010 SEDL9861 D1884217
X61A7469 A5752642 VAEF6708
MMDV6326 GYB94755 PIN72337

IMPORTANT!
HERE ARE YOUR 9 EXCLUSIVE PRIZE CLAIM NUMBERS

trants know they are being judged on the quality of their submission, they have to spend time preparing it. Sweepstakes, on the other hand, may require just minutes or maybe even seconds to enter. For this reason, it is not at all unusual to get 20, 50, or even 100 times the number of entries in a sweepstakes than in a contest of skill.

2. A contest of skill has minimal appeal to large segments of the market. For example, game contestants who are required to write a 25-word statement believe (from what fo-

ILLUSTRATION 5 ***(concluded)***

TEN MILLION DOLLARS!
OVER 85,000 PRIZES!
T-45a
SERIES

IF YOU RETURN THE WINNING NUMBER BY OCT. 26, 1985...

J. W. FEINMAN
SHALL BE PAID A FULL
TEN MILLION DOLLARS!
OUR BIGGEST WINNER EVER!

TEN MILLION DOLLARS RETURN BEFORE OCT.26 GUARANTEED

J. W. FEINMAN
is the GUARANTEED WINNER of TEN MILLION DOLLARS only if the enclosed entry is the grand prize winner and is returned before the date on seal at left.

Lift SEAL and affix to Entry-Order Card before date imprinted on this seal

WINNER TO BE ANNOUNCED
ON NBC TELEVISION'S TONIGHT SHOW

AVI
J. W. Feinman
870 V N. Plaza
New York, NY 10016

J. W. Feinman, now residing in New York, NY is hereby designated as a potential recipient of a full TEN MILLION DOLLARS in guaranteed annual payments of $333,333.00.

Financial guarantees have been provided by American Family Publishers for the full payment of this history-making award, and the aforementioned J. W. Feinman is, in fact, guaranteed the FULL TEN MILLION DOLLARS if the enclosed entry is Grand Prize Winner and is returned before the date on the special Gold Seal above. In this case, the annual payments will be made to J. W. Feinman's New York bank account or any bank account of J. W. Feinman's own choosing.

URGENT: J. W. Feinman can receive this Ten Million Dollar Prize ONLY IF the ADDRESS LABEL entry below is returned before the Gold Seal deadline. Otherwise, J. W. Feinman would forfeit all claim to this prize, and the entire TEN MILLION DOLLARS would have to be awarded to someone else.

PERSONAL PRIZE CLAIM NUMBERS
THE FOLLOWING NINE PRIZE CLAIM NUMBERS HAVE BEEN ISSUED SOLELY AND EXCLUSIVELY TO
J. W. FEINMAN

JT7H9010	SEDL9861	D1884217
X6IA7469	A5752642	VAEF6708
MMDV6326	GYB94755	PIN72337

RETAIN FOR YOUR RECORDS

President

08504-45-4-5/1-B

Courtesy of American Family Publishers.

cus groups tell us) that the prize will be awarded to an English teacher, a college student who is adept at writing, or an advertising copywriter. They don't believe that their general ability to communicate will allow them to effectively compete against people they regard as professionals.

3. There are significant postpromotion problems with contests. If someone in a contest has spent hours preparing an entry and another entry wins, the immediate reaction is to get a letter from his or her priest, English teacher,

and/or lawyer, or a testimonial from any number of people to state that the entry he or she sent in is better. Not only is such "white mail" time-consuming and expensive, but it leaves the losing entrants—which are obviously the vast majority—with a bad feeling about the sponsoring company. Obviously, this is a severe limitation.

4. There can be no ties in a contest of skill. Because all ties must be awarded duplicate prizes, contests are difficult to budget. Ties cannot be broken by a drawing because this would introduce the element of chance, thus making the game a lottery. (See Chapter 3 for a discussion of elimination of ties.)

Generally speaking, a contest does not do as well as a sweepstakes in generating proofs of purchase. This surprises many marketers because proof of purchase can be required in a contest of skill. However, since a sweepstakes may generate 20 times the number of entries as a contest, even if the contest gets 100 percent proof of purchase and the sweepstakes gets only 50 percent, the net proof of purchase is still greater with a sweepstakes. But contests still account for 5 percent or more of all prize promotions. Recipe contests utilizing the sponsor's ingredients have been successful; however, judging a contest of this kind is expensive. Another good use of contests was the unique promotion of Bill Adler's runaway best seller, *Who Killed the Robins Family* (see Chapter 4). The contest involved a mystery book in which the winner received a $10,000 reward for solving the mystery. The criteria for judging this innovative contest are outlined in the rules shown in Illustration 6.

In addition, contests can be effective when you want a very specialized audience to think favorably about your product. For example, Ventura recently conducted an offer for a textbook manufacturer who wanted to reach English professors. We sent out review copies of the book accompanied by a contest that asked respondents to write a brief essay: "In one hundred words or less, why do you believe this textbook could be a true breakthrough in teaching English?"

Here we were talking to people who are used to writing. They are also people who the sponsor wants to spend considerable

ILLUSTRATION 6 *Who Killed the Robins Family* Entry Form

The official rules for the *Who Killed the Robins Family* contest carefully outlined the criteria used to select the winner.

HERE ARE THE RULES FOR THE CONTEST

To enter, use ordinary paper. Make sure your name and address are clearly printed at the top of each page of your entry. Print or type your answers to the following *five* questions, for *each* of the *eight* members of the Robins family (Tyler Robins, Evelyn Robins, Marshall Robins, Libby (Robins) Pittman, Lewis Robins, James Robins, Cynthia Robins and Candace Robins):

1. Who was the killer?
2. Where did the murder take place?
3. When did the murder happen?
4. How was the victim killed?
5. Why was the victim killed?

Answer all questions in the order given, for each member of the family, one family member at a time. Each set of five answers must be clearly identified as relating to a single victim. Only entries with complete answers to all five questions for each of the victims are eligible for the prize. Mail your entry plus 50¢ processing fee (cash, check or money order), to: VENTURA ASSOCIATES, INC., P.O. Box 505, Lowell, Indiana 46356. Enter as often as you wish, but each entry must be mailed in a separate envelope, and must be accompanied by the 50¢ processing fee. All entries must be received by April 15, 1984.

Entries will be reviewed by VENTURA ASSOCIATES, INC., an independent judging organization whose decisions will be final. The correct answers, as determined by the authors, are based on clues found in the book. These answers are being held in a sealed vault pending the final date of the contest. If more than one (or no) completely correct solution is received, the final winning entry will be determined by the best answers to the questions "Why was the victim killed?" for each of the eight members of the Robins family. Best answers will be determined first by correctness. Answers will then be evaluated by the authors for logic, clarity of expression, creativity and neatness.

The winner of the $10,000 prize will be notified by mail on or before May 2, 1984, and the winner and the winning solution will be announced at the American Booksellers Association convention in Washington, D.C., on May 28, 1984. Contestants do not have to be present to win. The $10,000 prize will be awarded on or before June 10, 1984. No substitutions for the prize will be allowed. Any and all applicable taxes are the responsibility of the winner. The winner may be asked to sign a statement of eligibility and the winner's name and likeness may be used for publicity purposes. Entries are the property of William Morrow and Company, Inc. The contest is open to residents of the United States, eighteen years of age or older. Employees and their families of William Morrow and Company, Inc., Bill Adler Books, Inc., the Hearst Corporation, their respective affiliates and advertising agencies, VENTURA ASSOCIATES, INC., and the authors and their families, are not eligible. This contest is void where prohibited or restricted by law. All federal, state and local laws and regulations apply. For the name of the contest winner, send a stamped, self-addressed envelope to: Robins Family Winner, P.O. Box 632, Lowell, Indiana 46356.

To receive a copy of the authors' solution to the mystery, send a stamped, self-addressed envelope and 25¢ for handling to: Robins Family Solution, P.O. Box 709, Lowell, Indiana 46356. Requests for solutions will not be fulfilled before May 28, 1984, or later than May 28, 1986.

The $10,000 prize will be awarded for what is, in the sole determination of the judges, the *best* solution. Therefore, even if you're not 100% sure you're right, you still might come closest and win the $10,000!

Courtesy of William Morrow & Co.

time looking at a new product and thinking about it in a favorable way.

PUZZLES

There are other lesser known types of prize offers. One of these is called the puzzle club. This is not a promotion device you would use to increase sales.

In fact, the puzzle club is a business in itself. Remember, in a contest, consideration can be present when chance is not. We begin with a seemingly easy puzzle. For example, a puzzle club might show a picture of President Lincoln and give the clue: "He was born in a log cabin. Who was this president?" There would be a minimum 25-cent entry fee, but larger amounts would be accepted depending on how much the person wanted to win: for example, a $1 entry fee to win $1,000, $5 to win $5,000, and $8 to win a car. The consumer is told that there are likely to be ties, and if there are, a tiebreaker event will follow.

Sometimes consumers are excited by this device because they feel they know all about the presidents. However, the contests to break the ties become progressively harder. So, in tiebreaker round two there might be some obscure question about Franklin Delano Roosevelt. By tiebreaker five, the puzzle entrants are expected to read a 32-page booklet and answer such obscure questions as, "What is the name of the fifth President of Uganda's first son?" This device is of interest to prize promotion people because there may be a way to use just some of its elements—those that involve the people you want to reach.

INCENTIVE PROGRAMS

Prize promotions also have a prominent place in trade offers. In Chapter 4 we talk about display contests in which people are offered opportunities to build a display.

One type of offer that has recently become popular with sales forces is called a "sweepcentive." This type of offer combines the best features of a sweepstakes with the best features of an incentive program (see Illustration 7).

Most incentive programs have a significant limitation in that they usually require an open-ended budget. If a person is given points based on a certain amount of sales—for example, one point for every dollar in sales—there is always a question in the marketer's mind about how much money the salesperson can generate. Furthermore, sales incentive programs often lead to complaints from salespeople about inequities in the size and profitability of territories or the potential of customer lists. Also, a salesperson may be discouraged by the difficulty of achieving a major goal and set his or her sights too low. They may flip through the big catalog of incentive prizes and say, "Gee, all I have to do is increase my sales 10 percent and I will get this nice pen and pencil set. But to get the mink coat, which I'd really like to get for my wife, I have to increase my sales 3,000 percent. That's just impossible!"

ILLUSTRATION 7 Two Ways to Prosper, St. James Court

Adding a sweepstakes to a conventional prize point incentive program has proven to be an outstanding way to motivate salespeople to extraordinary effort.

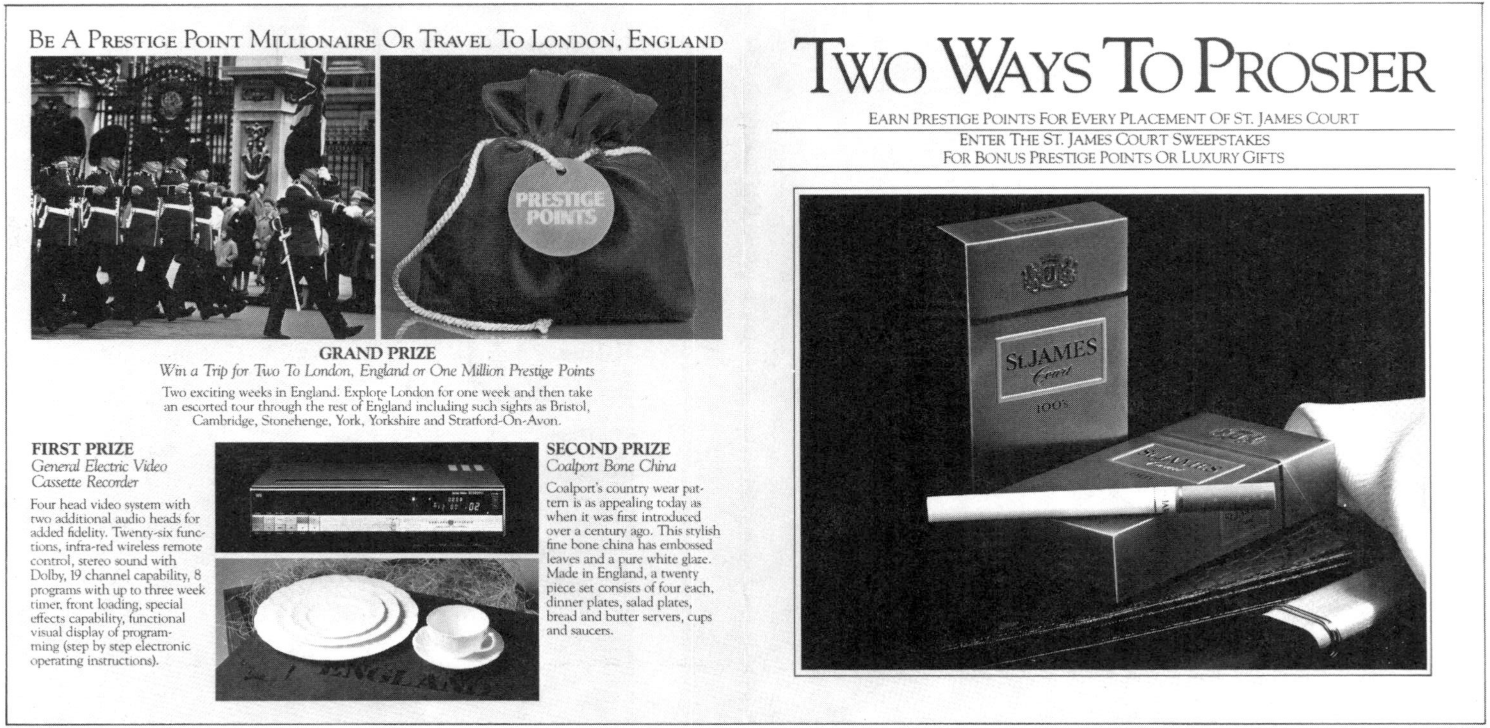

BE A PRESTIGE POINT MILLIONAIRE OR TRAVEL TO LONDON, ENGLAND
PRESTIGE POINTS
GRAND PRIZE
Win a Trip for Two To London, England or One Million Prestige Points
Two exciting weeks in England. Explore London for one week and then take an escorted tour through the rest of England including such sights as Bristol, Cambridge, Stonehenge, York, Yorkshire and Stratford-On-Avon.
FIRST PRIZE
General Electric Video Cassette Recorder
Four head video system with two additional audio heads for added fidelity. Twenty-six functions, infra-red wireless remote control, stereo sound with Dolby, 19 channel capability, 8 programs with up to three week timer, front loading, special effects capability, functional visual display of programming (step by step electronic operating instructions).
SECOND PRIZE
Coalport Bone China
Coalport's country wear pattern is as appealing today as when it was first introduced over a century ago. This stylish fine bone china has embossed leaves and a pure white glaze. Made in England, a twenty piece set consists of four each, dinner plates, salad plates, bread and butter servers, cups and saucers.
TWO WAYS TO PROSPER
EARN PRESTIGE POINTS FOR EVERY PLACEMENT OF ST. JAMES COURT
ENTER THE ST. JAMES COURT SWEEPSTAKES
FOR BONUS PRESTIGE POINTS OR LUXURY GIFTS
St. JAMES
Court
100's

Courtesy of Brown and Williams Tobacco Corp.

ILLUSTRATION 8 Best Buy Brands Game Cards: (not scratched off; scratched off)

Lever Brothers included a game piece that could be worth $1,000 with a $1 refund. The refund required purchase, while the sweepstakes did not.

Courtesy of Lever Brothers.

The sweepcentive addresses this problem by giving the salespeople one entry in the sweepstakes for each unit of performance; therefore, the more they sell, the better their chance to win. The theory is that the *certainty* of a smaller prize is not always as appealing as the *possibility* of a huge prize.

In short, prize promotions are really a whole catalog of different types of offers, and the names should not be used interchangeably. The important thing is to use the appropriate one for the specific occasion rather than reject any of them out of hand. And, of course, you should always be alert for an opportunity to use these devices in combination with other promotions; for example, a sweepstakes/refund in which a consumer is offered a guaranteed refund if they enter a sweepstakes with a proof of purchase but no refund if they enter the sweepstakes with a 3 × 5 card without the proof of purchase (see Illustration 8). The combination of two promotional devices will usually yield a greater result than can be achieved by using two of these devices separately.

CHAPTER THREE

Legal Aspects of Prize Promotions

This book is not intended to make the reader an expert on the legal aspects of prize promotion. However, the legalities are such an integral part of the planning process that a summary and interpretation of federal and state laws is necessary to assist the reader in the planning, developing, and administering of a prize program.

The first thing a businessperson must be concerned with when considering a prize promotion is interpreting the myriad regulations governing sweepstakes, games, and other prize offers. An independent judging organization or outside counsel can usually handle all of the compliance regulations and will guide the businessperson through the areas that need attention. However, the businessperson must also understand the risks and how to deal with them.

It is essential not to run afoul of the lottery laws that govern prize promotion. A prize promotion must not be construed by any federal, state, or local regulatory agency to be a lottery. Federal regulations prohibit lotteries in all 50 states except for those sponsored by state governments. Essentially, a lottery has three elements: prize, chance, and consideration. In order to make an offer legal, the marketer must omit any *one* of these three elements.

Prize is the simplest to define. It is the award or gift that a person receives for winning. Obviously, this is the one element that cannot be omitted, or no one would participate.

Chance is the selection of the winner by a drawing or some other random method. In a contest, we eliminate chance because selection of the winner is based on a predetermined skill requirement.

Finally, *consideration* is the payment, purchase, or substantial performance required for entry. Today, we cannot require an entrant to buy a product in order to participate in an offer—the traditional rules that required the submission of a box top are no longer permitted. What *is* permitted is the submission of a box top *or* the name of the product written on a plain piece of paper.

The performance element of consideration can be a little trickier. In certain states the requirement that a participant visit the sponsor's place of business has been determined to be consideration. Yet the law itself has not changed drastically over the years; what has changed is its interpretation. Promotion experts understand the practical application and interpretation of the law as it is currently construed and acted on by regulatory agencies.

Interpretation is the key operative issue because regulators' interpretations of the various statutes vary widely. To make this situation more complex, state and federal laws are often different and frequently contradictory. For example, the federal lottery law prohibits states that have lotteries from promoting them through the mails, but there is no federal law that forbids broadcasting state lottery commercials on radio or television, even when the station's signals cross state lines.

It is important to understand how the statutes affect various types of prize promotions.

SWEEPSTAKES

Sweepstakes are legal. The requirement we must remove to differentiate a sweepstakes from a lottery is consideration. We can *request* consideration, but we cannot *require* it. That is why you often see the statement: "To enter, send a box top or a 3 × 5 card on which you have printed the name of the product in plain block letters." The card is considered an alternative to the proof of purchase. Generally, for purposes of the lottery law, consideration does not include the postage required to mail the entry blank, the effort of completing the form, or a trip to the store to answer a relatively easy question. Postage is not viewed as consideration because there is a third-party beneficiary—the money for the stamp doesn't go to the advertiser, it goes to the Post Office. Marketers stretch this interpretation to include telephone prize promotions in which a consumer enters by calling a 900 number, for which 50 cents is charged to the consumer's phone bill.

The following are examples of various interpretations of the lottery laws as they pertain to sweepstakes:

You may have noticed a sweepstakes announcement on a package or on a store display. The burst on the package announces a free entry form or game piece inside. Since you have to buy the package to obtain the entry form, all the elements of a lottery are present: prize, chance, and consideration. In order to remove the consideration factor, there must be a free entry op-

ILLUSTRATION 9 Jell-O Pudding Pops Box

Because they reach the consumer at the final decision-making moment, on-pack sweepstakes and in-pack games are powerful product movers.

Courtesy of General Foods Corporation.

tion. This is accomplished by saying on the burst: "No purchase required. See details on back." (See Illustration 9.) On the back of the package, additional copy states: "To obtain a free entry form, send a self-addressed, stamped envelope to . . ." In this same example, we must also add the line, "Residents of the state of Washington send unstamped, self-addressed envelope." Washington is an exception to the norm; the state of Washington has determined that postage is not a consideration for an entry, but it *is* consideration when requesting a *free* entry form. At any time Washington could change its law and decide to conform to the procedure generally accepted in other states; on the other hand, other states may decide to adopt the Washington rule.

ILLUSTRATION 10 Penthouse 1983 Dream Car Sweepstakes

By including appropriate questions on the entry form, it is easy to obtain important demographic information along with sweepstakes entries.

PENTHOUSE 1983 DREAM CAR SWEEPSTAKES
Official Entry Form

Age	Household (Family) Income	Car Ownership (Household)
	__Under $15,000	Domestic Car
__18-24	__$15,000-$19,999	__(bought new)
__25-34	__$20,000-$24,999	Imported Car
__35-49	__$25,000-$34,999	__(bought new)
__50 or over	__$35,000 or over	

Please Print

NAME ____________________ AGE___

ADDRESS ____________________

CITY ____________ STATE____ ZIP______

Courtesy of Penthouse International, Ltd.

A sweepstakes entry form is sometimes used to obtain information from an entrant. Such requests could range from demographic information to the entrant's opinions. However, if the participant must invest an excessive amount of time to provide the answers, this could be deemed consideration (see Illustration 10).

Does all this sound like a legal morass? If so, you may be surprised to learn that, with the help of a sweepstakes administration expert and a competent attorney, there is probably less risk in a sweepstakes than in a coupon or premium offer.

CONTESTS

In this prize format we can require consideration, and it can be the purchase of the product. However, we must remove chance

ILLUSTRATION 11 Call It Culligan Contest, Free Entry Blank

In order to make a contest of skill valid—a condition that allows you to require purchase for participation—you must eliminate all elements of chance.

Free Entry Blank

Call It Culligan® CONTEST

Read the rules and full details inside this entry booklet. Then, submit your entry for one of the 48 exciting free prizes.

Turn On Your Creative Power! You Could Win An Exotic Vacation For Two In The Bahamas Or One Of 47 Other Valuable Prizes.

You'll find the complete rules and contest tips on the other side of this entry blank.

MAIL YOUR ENTRY TO:
Call It Culligan Contest
P.O. Box 517,
Lowell, Indiana 46356.
All entries must be received no later than May 21, 1985.

DESCRIBE YOUR WATER SCENE AND CAPTION HERE: (REMEMBER TO CALL IT CULLIGAN.)

Your Name
Address
City, State, Zip
Phone Number (Area Code)
Your Nearest Culligan Dealer:

Call It Culligan.

Contest Rules

1 On an Official Entry Form, write legibly your most original way to replace water with Culligan. (Example: I feel better after a warm Culligan bath.)

You may support your entry with pictures or art work on one sheet of paper no larger than 8½" x 11". Be sure your name, address and zip are written legibly on each piece of paper. Ability to draw does not count toward a prize. The originality, humor and appropriateness of the idea are all that count.

2 Mail your entry to: Call It Culligan Contest, P.O. Box 517, Lowell, IN 46356, or use envelope available. Enter as often as you like, but mail each entry separately. No purchase is necessary to enter.

Entries must be received no later than May 21, 1985.

3 Entries will be judged based on the following criteria:

Originality	60%
Appropriateness	20%
Humor	20%

Winners will be determined by VENTURA ASSOCIATES, INC., an independent judging organization whose decisions are final.

4 No duplicate winners. No substitution for prizes may be made other than necessary due to availability. Winners will be notified by mail and will be required to sign, and return an affidavit of eligibility within 21 days of date on notification. Grand Prize Trips must be taken between June 1 and December 31, 1985, subject to availability. All slogans submitted become the property of Culligan International and may be reprinted without permission or compensation.

5 Contest open to residents of the United States 21 years of age or older. Employees of Culligan International, their dealers and distributors, their respective advertising and production agencies, VENTURA ASSOCIATES, INC. and their immediate families are not eligible. No purchase required. Void where prohibited by law. All federal, state and local rules and regulations apply. Taxes are the responsibility of winners. Winners' names will be available at participating Culligan dealers within 90 days of conclusion of the contest.

Printed in U.S.A. 8648-74

Courtesy of Culligan U.S.A.

and substitute skill. The skill factor must be quite real and not just a subterfuge. Unless you are a mathematician, guessing the number of beans in a jar is not skill. Unless you are a professional handicapper, guessing the score in advance of an athletic competition is not a skill.

The majority of contests of skill involve either writing a jingle, solving a puzzle, writing a 25-word statement, completing a rhyme, or creating a recipe. For each one of these contests we must establish rigid criteria for judging and inform the potential contestant of them. These criteria might include originality, appropriateness, and creativity (see Illustration 11). We cannot permit ties in a contest of skill because we would have to give duplicate prizes, so we can refine our rules by weighting the criteria. For instance, originality might count 50 percent, while appropriateness might be weighted at only 10 percent. Another method for breaking ties is by using second and third rounds—and more if necessary—of tiebreaking questions. Tiebreakers must be the same type as the original contest. For example, you cannot follow up a jingle-writing contest of skill with a tiebreaker that requires solving a puzzle.

GAMES

Games are the quintessential continuity promotion. If you are looking for repeat purchases and repeat traffic, this is the prize promotion for you. Generally, a game falls under the same set of legal guidelines as does a sweepstakes. In fact, it really is a sweepstakes with continuity. And like a sweepstakes, we cannot require purchase so we must make game pieces available on request. This may involve passing them out to consumers who come into an outlet and don't make a purchase or sending them to people who send in a self-addressed, stamped envelope (see Illustration 12).

Games are the ultimate "predetermined winner" sweepstakes. Certain game pieces are already winners and have been "seeded" into the game pieces put into circulation. This is accomplished under the supervision of the sweepstakes administrator in the same manner as a random drawing; that is, procedures are employed to ensure that everyone participates under the same odds.

In addition, fraud detectors must be employed. Because many games have valuable high-end prizes, a game piece worth $100,000 could become a fraud inducement. The independent judging organization, working closely with qualified printers, ensures against misredemption caused by counterfeiting. There are many different techniques employed to prevent fraudulent entries, and they may change according to the construction of the game piece. Examples of different types of game pieces are scratch-offs, ruboffs, sealed-in-envelopes, and sealed and perforated lift-tabs. Some games are self-contained, and some employ a saver sheet. Lucky number promotions and match-and-win games come under this category too (see Illustration 13).

ILLUSTRATION 12 Win the World on TWA Game Cards (not scratched off; scratched off; official rules and entry form)

This game had TWA flying high. A trip for two to anywhere TWA flies was the low-end prize; the grand prize was a free trip for two every year for life.

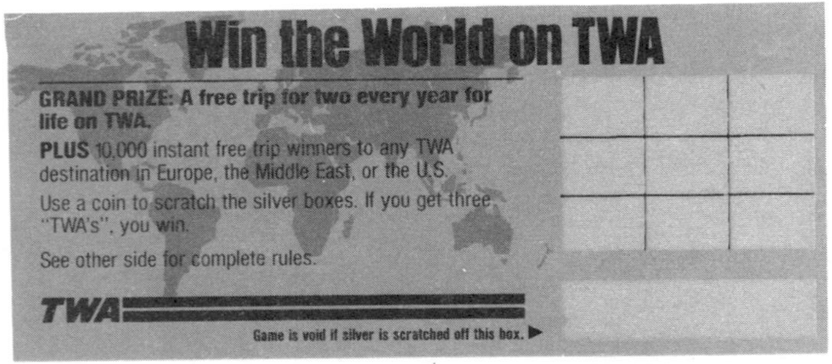

Win the World on TWA
GRAND PRIZE: A free trip for two every year for life on TWA.
PLUS 10,000 instant free trip winners to any TWA destination in Europe, the Middle East, or the U.S.
Use a coin to scratch the silver boxes. If you get three "TWA's", you win.
See other side for complete rules.
TWA
Game is void if silver is scratched off this box.

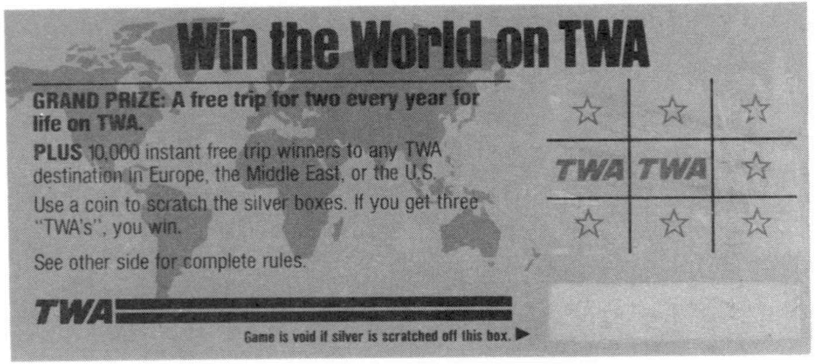

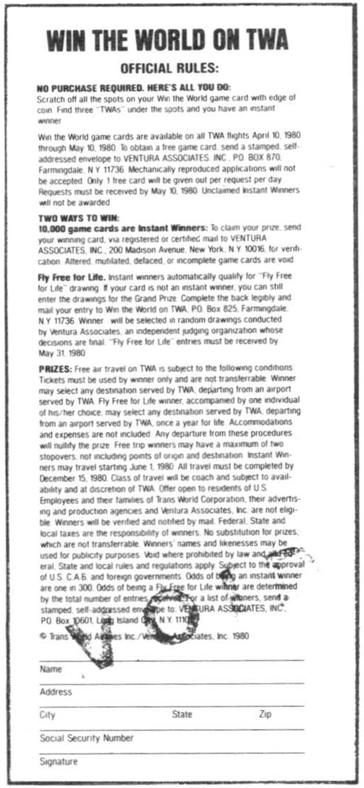

WIN THE WORLD ON TWA

OFFICIAL RULES:

NO PURCHASE REQUIRED. HERE'S ALL YOU DO: Scratch off all the spots on your Win the World game card with edge of coin. Find three "TWAs" under the spots and you have an instant winner.

Win the World game cards are available on all TWA flights April 10, 1980 through May 10, 1980. To obtain a free game card, send a stamped, self-addressed envelope to VENTURA ASSOCIATES, INC., P.O. BOX 870, Farmingdale, N.Y. 11736. Mechanically reproduced applications will not be accepted. Only 1 free card will be given out per request per day. Requests must be received by May 10, 1980. Unclaimed Instant Winners will not be awarded.

TWO WAYS TO WIN:
10,000 game cards are Instant Winners: To claim your prize, send your winning card, via registered or certified mail to VENTURA ASSOCIATES, INC., 200 Madison Avenue, New York, N.Y. 10016, for verification. Altered, mutilated, defaced, or incomplete game cards are void.

Fly Free for Life. Instant winners automatically qualify for "Fly Free for Life" drawing. If your card is not an instant winner, you can still enter the drawings for the Grand Prize. Complete the back legibly and mail your entry to Win the World on TWA, P.O. Box 825, Farmingdale, N.Y. 11736. Winner will be selected in random drawings conducted by Ventura Associates, an independent judging organization whose decisions are final. "Fly Free for Life" entries must be received by May 31, 1980.

PRIZES: Free air travel on TWA is subject to the following conditions. Tickets must be used by winner only and are not transferrable. Winner may select any destination served by TWA, departing from an airport served by TWA. Fly Free for Life winner, accompanied by one individual of his/her choice, may select any destination served by TWA, departing from an airport served by TWA, once a year for life. Accommodations and expenses are not included. Any departure from these procedures will nullify the prize. Free trip winners may have a maximum of two stopovers, not including points of origin and destination. Instant Winners may travel starting June 1, 1980. All travel must be completed by December 15, 1980. Class of travel will be coach and subject to availability and at discretion of TWA. Offer open to residents of U.S. Employees and their families of Trans World Corporation, their advertising and production agencies and Ventura Associates, Inc. are not eligible. Winners will be verified and notified by mail. Federal, State and local taxes are the responsibility of winners. No substitution for prizes, which are not transferrable. Winners' names and likenesses may be used for publicity purposes. Void where prohibited by law and all Federal, State and local rules and regulations apply. Subject to the approval of U.S. C.A.B. and foreign governments. Odds of being an instant winner are one in 300. Odds of being a Fly Free for Life winner are determined by the total number of entries received. For a list of winners, send a stamped, self-addressed envelope to: VENTURA ASSOCIATES, INC., P.O. Box 10601, Long Island City, N.Y. 1110[illegible]

© Trans World Airlines Inc./Ventura Associates, Inc. 1980

Name

Address

City State Zip

Social Security Number

Signature

Reproduced by permission of Trans World Airlines, Inc.

ILLUSTRATION 13 Holly Farms The Great American Picnic Game Cards (game card (saver sheet); game piece, scratched off; game piece, not scratched off)

Saver sheets are often employed when there are many combinations available in a continuity game promotion. This enables players to see how close they are to a big prize.

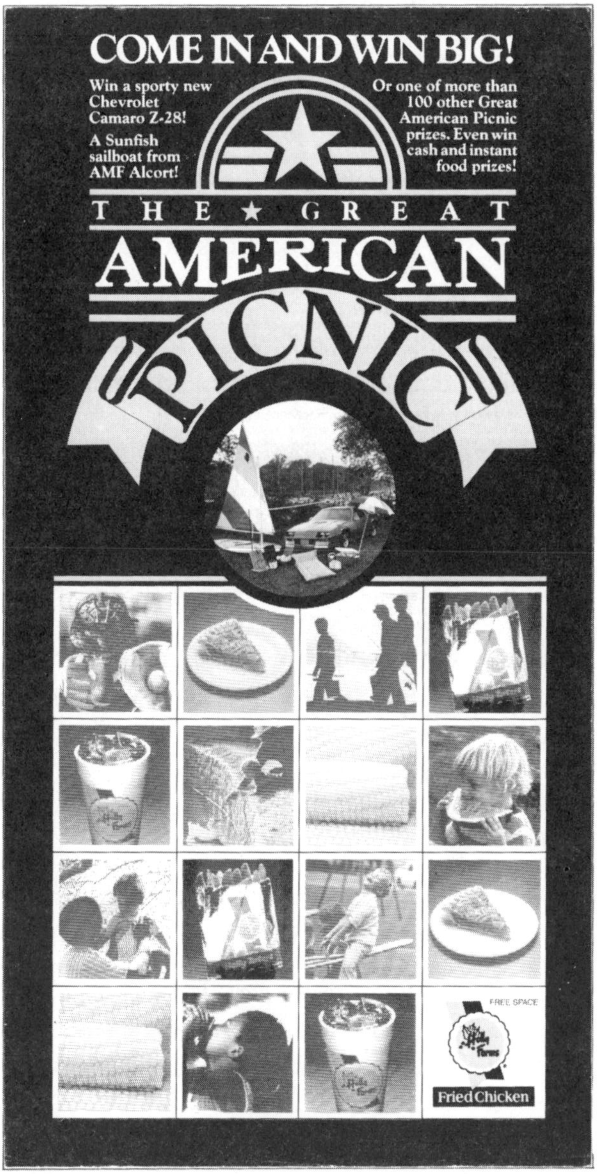

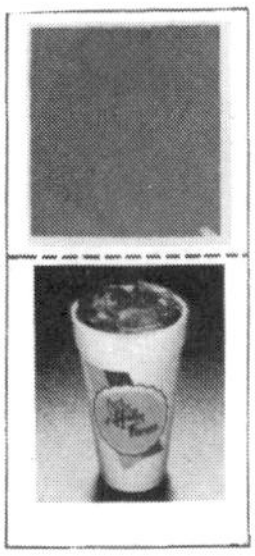

Courtesy of Holly Farms.

PROHIBITIONS AGAINST SWEEPSTAKES

Many states will not allow marketers of alcoholic beverages to run a sweepstakes. Other states may permit advertising but prohibit point-of-sale material. Local alcoholic beverage commissions are usually active in enforcing their rules and regulations. Some states even forbid nonalcoholic beverage sweepstakes on the premises of licensed alcohol retailers. In addition, some states have special laws and regulations regarding sweepstakes conducted by banks, dairies, and other specified industries. The Federal Alcohol, Tobacco and Fire Arms Commission has certain restrictions regarding the use of sweepstakes for tobacco products.

Florida, New York, and Rhode Island have registration requirements for sweepstakes but not for contests. Florida and New York require a surety bond or escrow account in the full amount of the value of the prizes as part of the registration. Since state and federal regulations can change at any time, these restrictions are only examples subject to updating by your sweepstakes administrator.

One additional word of caution: Rapid technological development constantly challenges our skills in the practical application of the lottery laws. The price scanners now popular at supermarket checkout counters offer many exciting opportunities for new kinds of sweepstakes and will surely test present-day lottery laws.

POSTAL AND FEDERAL TRADE COMMISSION REGULATION

The U.S. Postal Service has been assigned the task of regulating chance promotions whether or not your offer is sent through the mail. (This was a somewhat arbitrary governmental decision, just as firearms regulation somehow fell to the Bureau of Alcohol and Tobacco.) Clients often think that because their offer is either announced locally or distributed through circulars, they are exempt from the Postal Service lottery laws. However, the different types of offers outlined here are covered under Post Office Regulation 39 USC 3005. Furthermore, the Postal Service, until recently, provided a so-called letter of Post Office Approval.

Marketers frequently used these letters to defend their programs against state or local regulators. But the Postal Service recently announced that it would no longer provide this review and opinion service because letters were not being used as originally intended and this service was available from attorneys and specialists in prize promotions.

The purveyor of a prize promotion must also deal with the Federal Trade Commission—another major regulator of prize promotions. Much concern relates to the Federal Trade Commission Games Regulation Rules, which are encompassed in the commission's powers governing deceptive advertising. The FTC has also proposed guidelines for advertising of children's sweepstakes on television.

PROMOTIONS THAT ARE NO LONGER LEGAL

Before the days of stringent regulations, a wide variety of prize promotions were available to the marketer. Many enjoyed widespread and long-lived popularity with a public eager for new games to play and exciting prizes to win. Now, however, many of these prize promotions are illegal. Here is a partial list:

The Earliest Postmark Prize. According to the law, the element of chance is present in a prize promotion that offers a prize to a specified number of entries received by a stipulated deadline or postmarked by a certain date.

Guessing the Number of Beans in the Window. There was a time when guessing the number of beans in a window or the dollar value of coins in a jar was considered a feat of mathematics or a contest of skill. Today, this kind of contest may be judged to depend, at least in part, on chance. Federal lottery law applies to promotions in which the winner is chosen "in whole or in part" by lot or chance.

So-Called Easy-to-Win Contests. If the prize is to be awarded generally or arbitrarily, you cannot make it appear that the prize promotion is a contest of skill. The Justice Department has rules that so-called contests must require more skill than a rudimentary knowledge of arithmetic or a requirement that participants visit an advertiser's place of business to rack up prize points to be used later toward a purchase.

Guessing Games. Guesswork is "chance" in the eyes of the law. If guesswork is to be the major criteria for winning, then consideration must be eliminated to avoid a lottery violation.

Essay, Naming, and Limerick Contests. In order to be a true contest of skill, which is exempt from the rules governing lotteries, the criteria for choosing the winner must give the participants a real chance to demonstrate their skill. If that opportunity is absent, the contest may be perceived to involve the element of chance, and if, in addition, a purchase is required, the contest may be deemed to be a lottery.

A Home Visitor. If a prize is awarded to a consumer who happens to have the sponsor's product on hand when a representative randomly visits his or her home, the sponsor may be headed for a lottery violation.

The Landmark "Silverware Lottery" Case. The FTC ruled that a silverware dealer ran a lottery based on the following set of circumstances:

1. He distributed entry forms on which participants indicated their choice of flatware. The entry blank was then left behind for a prize drawing.
2. If the winner made a purchase later, the dealer gave him an additional prize.

There was no objection to the first element of the prize promotion, but in the second, consideration was involved and that made it a lottery.

Contingency Sale Prize. Some states consider it a lottery if the manufacturer or merchant offers a prize to a participant only if he or she provides them with the name of another potential customer.

Proof of Purchase and Number of Entries. You might be in for a lottery violation if your winner is based on the submission of the most wrappers, bottle caps or box tops, or other proofs of purchase. The Federal Trade Commission and several states consider the "Lucky Bottle Cap" promotion a lottery because the consumer would have to purchase a bottle of soda or other beverage in order to obtain the cap; in essence, consideration is involved. In a case like this you can avoid a lottery law violation by offering consumers free bottle caps on request.

In-Package Prizes. It is considered a lottery by the FTC if a manufacturer randomly places prizes, coins, lucky cards, coupons, or bonus certificates into certain packages of his product but not all of them, or even when all the packages contain a prize but the prizes are not of equal value.

The Prize Closet or Treasure Chest. If you distribute keys to purchasers, some of which will open a prize closet or treasure chest entitling the winner to receive all or some of the prizes, you would be running a lottery according to the FTC.

The businessperson's problem is to interpret the law and apply it to his or her particular type of program. Taking what may seem the easy way out by attempting to apply another prize promotion's rules to your program is fraught with danger. With 50 state jurisdictions and innumerable local regulators, there is always a contrary viewpoint, and, in the case of prize promotions, regulations are in a constant state of flux. Although prize promotion consultants are not attorneys and do not give legal advice, they do provide the benefit of daily experience in the practical application of lottery laws. This is essential because often there is no change in an actual law but merely a change in the interpretation or enforcement of the law.

One of the responsibilities of a professional judging organization is to stay on top of the changes in the law and its interpretation. They accomplish this not only by constant attention and vigilance but through the unique relationship they have with regulatory agencies. These agencies notify judging organizations of any changes, knowing that they, in turn, will notify the business community. Legal firms that specialize in lottery laws can be very helpful as well. A qualified sweepstakes judging organization will work with your own attorney to give him or her the benefit of practical judgment.

A LEGAL CHECKLIST

The following is a checklist of some legal requirements that must be covered in your sweepstakes rules:

- No Purchase Necessary
  This must be stated clearly and prominently.
- Alternate Means of Entry
  Where to send for *free* entry form or, if handwritten facsimile is allowed, its exact specifications and wording.
- List of Prizes
  The number of prizes being offered at each prize level, a description of each, and the cash substitute option (if any).
- Odds of Winning
  This may depend on the number of entries received or on the random seeding of winning game pieces, but you must state the odds correctly.
- Type of Sweepstakes
  Specify the type of game; i.e., random draw, predetermined winner, etc.
- Reasons for Disqualification
  Specify factors; i.e., altered, mutiliated, or incorrectly filled-out entry form, etc.
- Eligibility
  Specify all limits to eligibility; i.e., age, affiliation with related companies, etc.
- Limit on Entries
  There can be no limit on the number of entries, but only one entry is allowed per envelope.
- All Necessary Addresses
  Where to send completed entries, obtain free entry forms, and request list of winners.
- Void Clause
  List all states or localities where sweepstakes offer is void.
- Deadlines
  Deadlines for postmark, receipt of entries, and end date of sweepstakes.
- Limit of Sponsor's Liability
  Stipulate what the sponsor's responsibilities are and are not; i.e., taxes on prizes.

CHAPTER FOUR

What Sweepstakes Can and Cannot Do

One of the objectives of this book is to review a variety of marketing problems that can be solved efficiently through the use of prize promotions. We do not claim that prize promotion is the marketing panacea; however, there are times when there is no more efficient marketing solution. Also, a synergistic affect is often achieved when a prize promotion is used in conjunction with another promotion technique.

Many marketers fall in love with a particular marketing solution. Television filmmakers often believe that the TV commercial is the only way to move a product off the shelf, while many couponing people are convinced that couponing is the be all and end all. Our experience is that none of these solutions is effective in every instance.

Prize promotion is one more weapon that every marketer should have in his or her arsenal to help solve marketing problems. Just as good physicians know that penicillin is not always the answer to every disease, they nonetheless are aware of its properties so they can use it when appropriate.

Prize promotions suffer undeservedly from a bad image in the marketing community; they are not thought to be an upscale marketing tool. Because of this they are often underused. In some cases they are *inappropriately* used, and this perpetuates their unfavorable image. It is sad to hear a marketer say, "We don't use sweepstakes because we tried one for our product introduction, and it just didn't work." A good practitioner would understand that a sweepstakes may not have been an appropriate device for that particular product or in that particular instance.

Obviously, any discussion of what prize promotions can and cannot accomplish makes certain basic marketing assumptions—that the product is good, priced fairly, and meets a consumer demand. Advertising will sell a poor product only once. Sweepstakes can affect only a single sale. Basic marketing common sense tells us that a single sale of any product is inefficient, so we enter this discussion with the assumption that the product being sold meets the generally accepted standards of the marketplace.

The following are specific goals that prize promotions can attain.

BUILDING TRAFFIC

Prize promotion is the single most effective marketing technique for building traffic. McDonald's has consistently demonstrated that offering customers game cards that give them a chance to win a valuable prize is a powerful marketing tool that brings people to the restaurant. This game device will buy traffic at a lower cost per person than any other single method. Traditionally, people look at prize promotion as a traffic builder for fast-food restaurants, supermarkets, or gas stations. However, there are many other businesses in which traffic building is important and in which sweepstakes can be used.

Traffic building is obviously important to any retail business from a dry cleaner to a bank. But you have to be selective about the amount and kind of traffic desired. For example, a retail credit dealer, or even a bank, may say that they don't want to increase traffic unless it consists of people specifically interested in their service.

In Chapters Six and Seven we discuss several things that can be done to tailor an offer to people who will be particularly interested in purchasing your product. Sometimes this can be accomplished through media selection alone. Late in the 1960s, a new technique was developed to aid in the purchase process. It centers on getting people to do things that will create a sale without directly asking for an order. Nowhere is this better exemplified than in Revlon's CHAZ "Dream Machine" Sweepstakes. All the popular men's magazines carried an exciting ad featuring the CHAZ spokesman as well as the grand prize in the sweepstakes—a Lotus Turbo sports car (see Illustration 14). Hundreds of other exciting prizes were also offered. In addition, the ad had a game card insert with a scratch-off device. Entrants were invited to check the number revealed on the insert with the winning numbers on the displays in retail stores. People actually traveled for miles looking for a store with a winning number display. Many people took advantage of the write-in option for a facsimile of the display, and many dealers actually requested additional displays! This is not a common phenomenon, especially considering the universal cry of packaged good marketers: "I

ILLUSTRATION 14 CHAZ Ad with Game Card Insert, Revlon

An insert in a magazine ad permits "seeding"—making some participants instant winners, others solely sweepstakes entries. Inserts generally increase response significantly over on-page coupons.

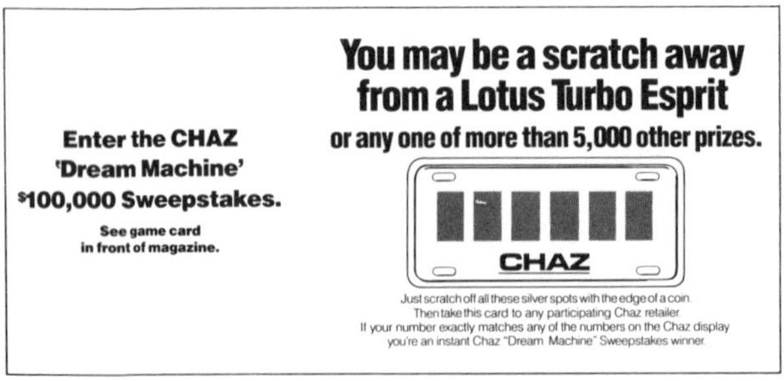

spend thousands of dollars on point-of-sale material and it sits in some store's back room!"

INCREASING DIRECT MAIL RESPONSE

Overlaying a sweepstakes on a direct mail offer has revitalized entire segments of the direct mail industry. It is not at all unusual to gain a 30 to 100 percent increase in orders by overlaying sweepstakes in a direct mail campaign. Many people know the direct mail success stories of *Readers Digest,* American Family Publishers, and Publisher's Clearing House. However, they often fail to recognize that most direct mailers, from small vitamin companies like Bio-Organic Brands to major upscale mailers like Home Box Office and specialized publications such as *Financial World,* have successfully used sweepstakes to increase direct mail response.

Legally, the mailer cannot require a purchase as a prerequisite to entering a sweepstakes; there must be what is known as a Yes/No option. The Yes/No option can be presented as follows: "YES, enter me in the sweepstakes and start my subscription to TENNIS magazine at just half the regular $17.94 subscription price. I get 12 issues for only $8.97! Bill me later." or "NO, enter me in the sweepstakes, but I do not want to subscribe to TENNIS magazine" (see Illustration 15).

The sophisticated marketer counts only the number of yes responses in determining the effectiveness of the offer. It is interesting to note that the no responses, or the nonbuyers, that were once considered just a cost of handling, are now, in fact, a profit center for many direct marketers. The no responses comprise a unique rentable mailing list. A mailer who rents this no list can cover not only the cost of handling such no responses but can actually make a profit.

INCREASING COUPON REDEMPTION

Sweepstakes can dramatically increase coupon redemption. To put it simply, a sweepstakes overlay to a standard cents-off cou-

ILLUSTRATION 15 *Tennis* Sweepstakes Entry Form

The Yes/No option on an order entry form is often the force that overcomes the inertia that keeps people from responding.

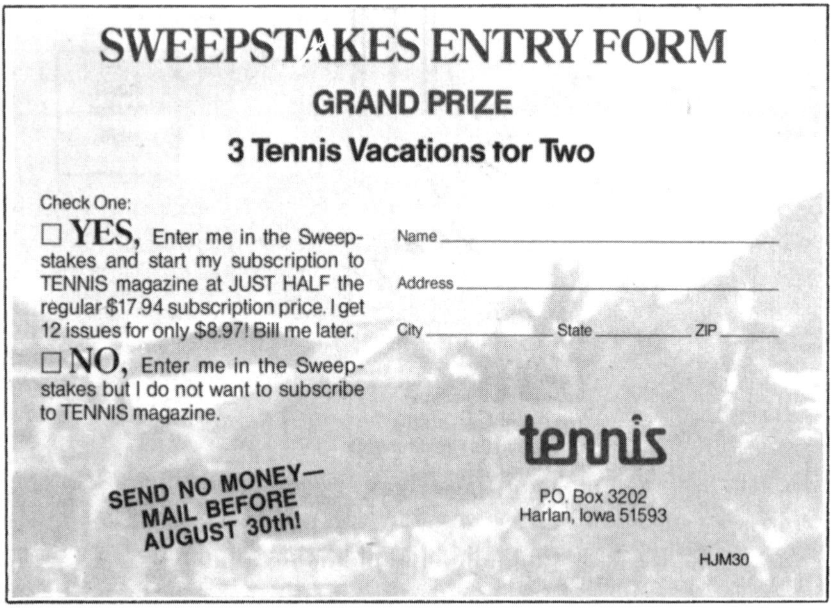

SWEEPSTAKES ENTRY FORM

GRAND PRIZE

3 Tennis Vacations for Two

Check One:

☐ YES, Enter me in the Sweepstakes and start my subscription to TENNIS magazine at JUST HALF the regular $17.94 subscription price. I get 12 issues for only $8.97! Bill me later.

☐ NO, Enter me in the Sweepstakes but I do not want to subscribe to TENNIS magazine.

Name ______

Address ______

City ______ State ______ ZIP ______

SEND NO MONEY—
MAIL BEFORE
AUGUST 30th!

tennis

P.O. Box 3202
Harlan, Iowa 51593

HJM30

Courtesy of Golf Digest/Tennis, Inc.

poning ad can produce a 30 percent lift in redemption levels (see Illustrations 16, 17, 17a, and 17b).

OBTAINING A DIFFICULT-TO-COMPLETE QUESTIONNAIRE

The marketer is often faced with the problem of gathering information from his consumers. He may want to obtain a demographic profile or the completion of a warranty card, or induce the consumer to fill out a long application such as a Diner's Club Card or a MasterCard application. Sweepstakes have been effective in all these cases. The requirement for entry could be the completion of the information section; therefore, the questionnaire might simply say, "Complete this questionnaire to be eligible to win in our sweepstakes" (see Illustration 18).

ILLUSTRATION 16 America's Greatest Athlete, Ocean Spray

A price-off coupon that becomes an entry in a sweepstakes will boost redemption rates significantly.

Team up with Ocean Spray®
and vote for your
favorite woman athlete.
You can help Ocean Spray support American women in sports by electing the most outstanding woman athlete of the past 25 years.
AND WIN A TRIP TO YOUR FAVORITE SPORTS EVENT.
Just complete the ballot below and you'll be automatically eligible to win two tickets to any sports event, anywhere in the world. Or you could win one of over 10,000 sweepstakes prizes.
Enter and vote as often as you like. Simply look for specially marked Ocean Spray bottles.
So cast your vote today and join Ocean Spray in bringing national recognition to this country's finest sportswoman. Plus, for every ballot received, Ocean Spray will make a donation to the Women's Sports Foundation.
WOMEN'S SPORTS FOUNDATION
A non-profit organization dedicated to the promotion, education and training of America's women in sports.
Candidates were selected from a list of internationally recognized American athletes by the Women's Sports Foundation and a panel of leading sports journalists.
GRAND PRIZE – A trip for two to the Sporting Event of your choice, anywhere in the world.
(10) 1st PRIZES – A NIKON Sports Binocular, plus a NIKON camera.
(350) 2nd PRIZES – A TIMEX® Sports Quartz™ watch.
(10,000) 3rd PRIZES – Women's Sports Foundation Fitness and Sports Resource Guide.
WOMEN'S SPORTS FOUNDATION
Ocean spray
Ocean spray
Good for You, America!
OCEAN SPRAY® "AMERICA'S GREATEST ATHLETE" OFFICIAL RULES.
It's Easy to Enter, Here's All You Do: 1. NO PURCHASE REQUIRED. To enter complete an official ballot found in Ocean Spray ads or on specially marked labels. Also enter the sweepstakes by completing and redeeming specially marked store coupons/ballots by 12/31/84. Coupons must be cleared and returned to the judging organization by March 31, 1985. You may also enter by hand printing your name, address, zip code and your choice for America's Greatest Woman Athlete on a plain piece of paper 3" x 5". Enter as often as you wish but each entry must be mailed separately. Select your choice for athlete and mail your entry to the Post Office Box listed for that athlete. All entries must be received by March 31, 1985. 2. Winners will be determined in random drawings conducted by VENTURA ASSOCIATES, INC., an independent judging organization whose decisions are final. Winners will be notified by mail. 3. Odds of winning are dependent upon the number of entries received. (Estimated sweepstakes entries – 1 million.) No duplicate prizes. Total cost of the Grand Prize is limited to $10,000. 4. Sweepstakes open to U.S. residents, except where prohibited by law. Not open to employees and their families of Ocean Spray, their advertising agencies and Ventura Associates, Inc. All Federal, State and local laws and regulations apply. 5. For a list of major prize winners send a stamped, self-addressed envelope to Ocean Spray Sweepstakes Winners List, P.O. Box WL642, Lowell, IN 46356.
Official Ballot/Entry Form
I vote for (check one):
☐ Mary Decker P.O. Box 518
☐ Billie Jean King P.O. Box 532
☐ Chris Evert Lloyd P.O. Box 615
☐ Martina Navratilova P.O. Box 686
☐ Wilma Rudolph P.O. Box 700
☐ ________ P.O. Box 755
Your write-in choice
Candidates were selected from a list of internationally recognized American Women Athletes by The Women's Sports Foundation and a nationwide panel of leading sports journalists.
Name
Street
City
State Zip
Mail your ballot to the P.O. Box listed for your choice to: America's Greatest Woman Athlete, P.O. Box ____ Lowell, IN 46356.
VOID
15¢ OFF
ANY SIZE OF OCEAN SPRAY® CRANAPPLE® OR CRAN-GRAPE®
Grocer, this coupon will be redeemed for 15¢ + 8¢ handling, provided • You receive a real sale of Ocean Spray Cranberries, Inc. product • You mail this coupon to P.O. Box 1364, Clinton, Iowa 52734 • You supply, on request, invoices proving sufficient stock purchases to cover coupons presented • Customer pays any sales tax. Void where prohibited, taxed, or restricted by law • Offer expires December 31, 1984. Limit one coupon per customer.
STORE COUPON
31200 113624
REDEEM NOW

Reproduced by permission of Ocean Spray Cranberries, Inc.

ILLUSTRATION 17 Mr. Clean's 25th Anniversary Trivia Sweepstakes Ad

A sweepstakes overlay to a coupon offer is effective when proof of purchase is requested.

MR. CLEAN
25th
ANNIVERSARY
CELEBRATE MR. CLEAN'S 25TH ANNIVERSARY
ENTER THE TV TRIVIA SWEEPSTAKES
SAVE 40¢ AND TAKE MR. CLEAN'S TV TRIVIA QUIZ
If you're stumped, see the special Mr. Clean display at participating stores for correct answers or see rule 2.
GRAND PRIZE-A VINTAGE LATE 50's T-BIRD
(Approx. Retail Value—$27,000) or $27,000 in cash
• 25 1st Prizes: RCA 45" Large Screen TV's (Approx. Retail Value—$3,000)
• 250 2nd Prizes: Trivial Pursuit™ board games (Approx. Retail Value—$35).
• 2,500 3rd Prizes: "The Complete Unabridged Super Trivia Encyclopedia" (Approx. Retail Value—$4.95)
• 25,000 4th Prizes: Two 50¢ Mr. Clean coupons
• Over 25,000 chances to win!
MR. CLEAN'S TV TRIVIA SWEEPSTAKES OFFICIAL RULES
No purchase necessary. Here's all you do:
1. Complete the official entry form, or on a plain piece of 3" X 5" paper hand print your name, address, zip code and the correct answers to the questions below.
Include with your entry the picture of Mr. Clean from the front label of any size of Mr. Clean (to remove label, soak bottle in hot water) or the words "MR. CLEAN 25th ANNIVERSARY" in plain block letters on a separate 3" X 5" piece of paper.
2. Enter as often as you wish but mail each entry separately in a hand addressed envelope no larger than 4½" x 7½" to: Mr. Clean 25th Anniversary Sweepstakes, P.O. Box 554, Lowell, IN 46356. Entries must be postmarked between June 15, 1984 and December 31, 1984 and received by January 15, 1985. To obtain answers to trivia questions, see our display at participating stores or send a stamped, self-addessed envelope to Mr. Clean Trivia Answers, P.O. Box 749, Lowell, IN 46356. Residents of the state of Washington ONLY need not affix postage to their self-addressed envelopes.
3. Winners will be determined in random drawings on or about January 16, 1985 from all entries received by January 15, 1985. Random drawings will be conducted under the supervision of VENTURA ASSOCIATES INC., an independent judging organization, whose decisions are final. Winners will be notified by mail. Major prize winners will be required to sign a statement of eligibility which must be returned within 21 days of date on notification. Only one winning entry per family. No substitution for prizes other than as offered or as may be necessary due to availability. Odds of winning are determined by the number of entries received by January 15, 1985 containing the correct answers. All prizes will be awarded. For a list of major prize winners, send a stamped, self-addessed envelope to Mr. Clean Winners List, P.O. Box 712, Lowell, IN 46356.
4. Sweepstakes open to residents of the United States. Employees and their families of Procter & Gamble, its affiliates, subsidiaries, retailers, advertising agencies and VENTURA ASSOCIATES, INC., are not eligible. Void where prohibited or restricted.
MR. CLEAN TV TRIVIA SWEEPSTAKES QUESTIONS AND ENTRY FORM
1. When Mr. Clean was introduced life was much simpler, especially for the Beaver. His worst problems could be solved by milk and cookies and some fatherly advice. Except for Wally's obnoxious friend
2. One of the better known TV dads of the late 50's and early 60's was Danny Thomas in a comedy called
3. In 1963, Mr. Clean introduced a new plastic bottle, and the whole country was watching two boys grow up on "The Adventures of Ozzie and Harriet". Their TV names were the same as in real life. Name them
4. Ralph made his living driving a bus, but what did old pal Norton do?
5. In what year did Mr. Clean make his national television debut?
1. ____ 2. ____ 3. ____ 4. ____ 5. ____
Name ____
Address ____
City ____ State ____ Zip Code ____
Mail completed entries to Mr. Clean 25th Anniversary Sweepstakes, P.O. Box 554, Lowell, IN 46356.
To obtain answers to the trivia questions, see official rules above.
6228MC
MANUFACTURER COUPON | NO EXPIRATION DATE
SAVE 25¢
WHEN YOU BUY ONE ANY SIZE MR. CLEAN
42829
CONSUMER: Don't embarrass your dealer; redeem this coupon ONLY by purchasing the brand size(s) indicated, with its value deducted from retail selling price. Coupon may not be reproduced. Void if transferred to any person, firm or group prior to store redemption. You pay any sales tax. Any other use constitutes fraud. LIMIT ONE COUPON PER PURCHASE.
DEALER: Your redemption signifies compliance with P&G Coupon Requirements dated 10/1/83. Free copy available by writing to PROCTER & GAMBLE, 2150 Sunnybrook Drive, Cincinnati, Ohio 45237. Send properly redeemed coupons to same address. Cash Value 1/100 of 1¢ 8407
25¢
PROCTER & GAMBLE
5 37000 24125
6284MC
MANUFACTURER COUPON | NO EXPIRATION DATE
SAVE 15¢
WHEN YOU BUY ONE ANY SIZE MR. CLEAN
42949
CONSUMER: Don't embarrass your dealer; redeem this coupon ONLY by purchasing the brand size(s) indicated, with its value deducted from retail selling price. Coupon may not be reproduced. Void if transferred to any person, firm or group prior to store redemption. You pay any sales tax. Any other use constitutes fraud. LIMIT ONE COUPON PER PURCHASE.
DEALER: Your redemption signifies compliance with P&G Coupon Requirements dated 10/1/83. Free copy available by writing to PROCTER & GAMBLE, 2150 Sunnybrook Drive, Cincinnati, Ohio 45237. Send properly redeemed coupons to same address. Cash Value 1/100 of 1¢ 8407
15¢
PROCTER & GAMBLE
5 37000 24115

Courtesy of Procter & Gamble.

ILLUSTRATION 17a Chock full o'Nuts $1,000,000.00 Golden Scoopstakes Consumer Advertisement with Coupon

This consumer ad utilized free-standing inserts and vividly portrayed the impact of an in-pack game. The customary Chock full o'Nuts Scoop was the game device.

Courtesy of Chock full o'Nuts Corporation.

ILLUSTRATION 17b Ocean Spray Go-Anywhere Sweepstakes, Coupon with Entry Blank

In this promotion, the coupon is an automatic entry. The theme ties into the product, and the graphics treat the sweepstakes and product equally.

Reproduced by permission of Ocean Spray Cranberries, Inc.

ILLUSTRATION 18 United Virginia Bank, Sweepstakes Entry and Guarantee of Acceptance

A sweepstakes can be an effective inducement to obtain information about an individual.

SWEEPSTAKES ENTRY AND

GUARANTEE OF ACCEPTANCE

This offer made exclusively to:

John D. Sample
35 Morrissey Blvd.
Boston, MA 02125

Please make any corrections to your name and address.

YOUR APPROVED LINE OF CREDIT IS $10,000.00

A United Virginia Bank Premier VISA Card has been reserved in your name, with a line of credit as indicated. You have already been approved for this Card. The form below is necessary for our records. Please fill it out completely and return it to us, so that we may issue your Card promptly. At the same time, we will enter your name in our Orient-Express Sweepstakes.

0001

United Virginia Bank

A. D. Robinson
Authorized Signature

☐ YES, I accept the new United Virginia Bank Premier VISA Card reserved in my name. Please enter me in the Sweepstakes.

Please print your name as you would like it to appear on your card.

First name ______ Initial ______ Last name ______

Social Security Number ____/____/____

Telephone: Home (___) ______

Telephone: Business (___) ______

Employer ______
(Indicate if self-employed or retired)

Employer's address ______

City ______ State ______ Zip ______

Your position ______

Annual income* ______

Applicant's Bank Reference: ______

*Do you have additional income you'd like us to consider?
(You do not have to disclose alimony, child support, separate maintenance income or its source unless you want us to consider it in connection with this application.)

Amount ______ Source ______

Mother's maiden last name (please print) ☐☐☐☐☐☐☐☐☐☐
(For security purposes)

Your signature ______

Date ______

Complete this section only if there is to be a co-applicant on this account.

Co-applicant's name ______
First name Initial Last name

Co-applicant's Social Security Number ____/____/____

Address ______

City ______ State ______ Zip ______

Telephone: Home (___) ______

Telephone: Business (___) ______

Co-applicant's employer ______

Employer's address ______

City ______ State ______ Zip ______

Annual income* ______ Source* ______

Co-applicant's signature ______

Date ______

This Guarantee of Acceptance must be completed and signed for our records, or your Premier VISA Card cannot be issued. (We will bill you later for your annual membership fee.)

☐ NO, I prefer to enter the Sweepstakes without accepting my United Virginia Bank Premier VISA Card.

Courtesy of United Virginia Bank.

STIMULATING PROGRAMMED LEARNING

An advertiser often has a difficult message to disseminate to a consumer. This may be because the message is complex or because the consumer starts with some preconceived notion. For example, *Psychology Today* was faced with a problem when media buyers believed that they knew all about the *Psychology Today* audience. Customarily, the magazine ran ads in publications that media buyers read, such as *Advertising Age.* However, their post-research showed that the ads were not read. The media buyers' response was, "Why do I need to read them? I know all about *Psychology Today.*" The problem was solved through the use of a sweepstakes. By simply changing the ad's headline, *Psychology Today* was able to get the information it required.

The reader was required to read the ad carefully and then answer certain questions, such as: "What is the average income of the *Psychology Today* reader?" The information was readily available in the ad. In fact, the correct answers to five questions could be found by reading the ad, and answering them qualified the media buyer for the opportunity to win a car. The opportunity to win a valuable prize became the incentive to read the ad (see Illustration 19). This device is called programmed learning—supply the reader with answers to your questions and offer them something in return (in this case, entry in a sweepstakes). The reader is challenged to learn the information you give them. And experience tells us that the incentive to win a valuable prize will motivate a reader to read not only an ad but a brochure and even an entire book!

REINFORCED PRODUCT OR SERVICE BENEFIT

In a contest of skill, we can ask consumers to write what it is they like about a particular product. This encourages them to think about the product in a favorable way. For example, in a sweepstakes we can make it a requirement of entry to list the three most important benefits that a consumer perceives in a product. In order to enter, the consumer is required to look over a

ILLUSTRATION 19 *Psychology Today* Car Contest

At both the consumer and trade levels, a sweepstakes can be used to reinforce product knowledge that will be instrumental in making a sale.

Give us the numbers, and we might give you the keys.

Index of Concentration: U.S. Adults = 100	Car Bought New in 1974	Imported Car Bought New	30,000 Mileage Past Year	Car Wax/Polish Used Past Year*	Regular Radials Bought New*	Used Camping-Vehicle Past Year
Psychology Today	( )	( )	( )	( )	( )	( )
Time	150	178	146	108	128	108
Newsweek	124	172	144	118	150	120
U.S. News & World Rept.	118	178	141	107	178	124
Harper's/Atlantic	97	230	123	64	97	56
New Yorker	155	226	128	112	197	61
Sat. Review World	161	210	132	71	105	34
Sports Illustrated	158	138	161	121	129	136
Playboy	121	163	139	125	121	125
Esquire	166	194	131	122	149	93

SEND TO: Psychology Today "Car Contest" Ventura Associates, 40 East 49th Street, New York, N.Y. 10017 For correct answers consult W. R. Simmons 1974/1975 Magazine Audience Report, or call (212) 661-8200.

NAME: COMPANY: POSITION: ADDRESS: PHONE:

All it takes to win this new car is a sharp pencil, and some sharp answers.

If you work for an ad agency, or in the marketing or advertising department of an advertiser, just fill in the blanks for Psychology Today in the comparison chart, and send your answers to:

Psychology Today "Car Contest," at the address on the coupon.

If your answers are correct and postmarked by 4/20/76, you get a chance to win a Chevrolet Monte Carlo* with air conditioning, AM/FM radio and vinyl roof. The winner will be determined by a random drawing from all correct answers.

We'll give you a clue: more PT readers buy new cars than the readers of just about every other major magazine.

In just about every case, whether it involves automobile purchases, travel or community activities, PT readers are at or near the top of the list.

That's because PT readers know what they want in life and go after it. They live their dreams today, not tomorrow.

The more you know about PT readers, the more you'll know you should be a PT advertiser.

PT readers live their dreams today, not tomorrow.

Psychology Today

A Ziff-Davis Publication

*Car delivered within the contiguous continental United States at dealer nearest winner's legal residence. Freight charges, sales taxes and license fees not included.

All entries must be received by April 20, 1976. No substitution for prize offered. Winner selected in random drawing from all correct entries received by Ventura Associates, an independent judging organization. If no correct entries are received, a winner will be selected from all entries. Final authority on correct answers is the W.R. Simmons 1974/1975 Magazine Audience Report. Employees of Ziff-Davis Publishing Company and its advertising and judging agencies are not eligible. Offer void wherever prohibited or restricted by law. All Federal, state and local laws apply. Multiple entries void participation. Decision of the judges is final. Payment of Federal, state and local taxes imposed on the prizewinner is the sole responsibility of the prizewinner. For the name of the winner, send a separate stamped, self-addressed envelope to Ventura Associates, 40 East 49th St., New York, New York 10017.

Courtesy of *Psychology Today.*

list of benefits and then simply indicate his or her choices. This reinforces the benefits that consumers already believe are important to them (see Illustration 20).

BUILDING A MAILING LIST

Sweepstakes are a valuable tool in building a mailing list. This can be accomplished by including a sweepstakes entry in an advertisement, in a direct mail piece, or within the product package. So, if you are unsuccessful in garnering warranty cards or if the product is priced at a level where warranty cards would be inappropriate, you can place a sweepstakes entry within your product package and soon fill a mailing list of your own customers.

IMPROVING DISPLAY COMPLIANCE

The trade's willingness to use a display is a function of how much that display will help them sell the product. The trade frequently sees a contest or sweepstakes display as a powerful, product-moving tool. Therefore, the solution to a frustrating marketing problem—getting the store to use the display (what we call "display compliance")—can be solved through the use of contests and sweepstakes.

MOTIVATING SALESPEOPLE AND REWARDING OUTSTANDING PERFORMANCE

There are a multitude of promotion devices that can be used to motivate a sales force, but none is more effective than a sweepstakes in which the trade is offered a chance in the sweepstakes for every unit of sale, rather than a point-gathering system that is typical of most incentive programs. The power of this device lies in the fact that many people would rather have the chance to win a trip to Europe than the certainty of getting a pen and pencil set.

ILLUSTRATION 20 Greenview Greenstakes Entry Blank and Rules

A classic programmed learning effort. The answers to the questions on this entry form, which was attached to bags of Greenview Lawn Care Product, could be found right on the bag.

ENTER TODAY!

To become eligible for one of the Great Green Prizes, send this entry form before June 8, 1984. ALL BLANKS MUST BE FILLED IN TO BE ELIGIBLE.

Name ____________________
Please print

Address ____________________

City ____________________ State ________ Zip ________

Retailer where Greenview could be or was purchased:

Retailer Name ____________________ City ________

$5,000 CASH BONUS PRIZE

¿GREAT GREEN QUESTION?

IF YOU SHOULD WIN THE GRAND PRIZE, WIN AN ADDITIONAL $5,000 FOR CORRECTLY COMPLETING THE BLANKS BELOW:
(The answers are on the back of the bag.)

Green Power® is a specially developed __ - _ - _ formula lawn food that will build and maintain a sturdy luxuriant and beautiful lawn. It can be applied _______ during the growing season and provides sustained feeding without burning, when applied as directed.

DETACH AND MAIL TO: GREENSTAKES, P.O. BOX 692, LOWELL, IN 46356

OFFICIAL SWEEPSTAKES RULES

No purchase required, here's all you do:

1. Complete the official entry form, or on a plain piece of paper 3″ x 5″ hand print your name, address, zip, name of your Greenview retailer and the answer to the question above.

2. Enter as often as you wish but mail each entry separately to: **Greenstakes, P.O. Box 692, Lowell, IN 46356.** Entries must be received by June 8, 1984. Winners will be determined in random drawings conducted by Ventura Associates, Inc., an independent judging organization whose decisions are final. Winners will be notified by mail and may be required to sign and return an eligibility statement within 21 days of date on notification. Winners names and likenesses may be used for publicity purposes. Taxes are the responsibility of winners.

3. Sweepstakes open to residents of the United States except employees and their families of Lebanon Chemical Corporation, their distributors, retailers, advertising and promotion agencies and Ventura Associates are not eligible. Void where prohibited by law. All Federal, State and local rules and regulations apply. No substitution for prizes other than as offered or as may be necessary due to availablility, no duplicate prizes.

4. The $10,000 grand prize winner will receive a $5,000 bonus award for correctly answering the bonus question. The 10,000 fifth prizes will be awarded as follows: 4,000 from all entries received by March 10; 3,000 from all entries received between March 11 and April 10; 3,000 from all entries received from April 11 to May 10, 1984. Odds of winning are determined by the total number of entries received.

For a list of major prize winners send a stamped, self-addressed envelope to: Greenview Greenstakes Winners List, P.O. Box 541, Lowell, IN 46356.

Courtesy of Greenview Products and Lebanon Chemical Corporation.

Every businessperson knows the value of incentive programs. They can work for just about every business, product, or service at both the wholesale and retail level. The power of incentive programs can be magnified many times when run in conjunction with a consumer promotion.

In an attempt to reduce customer dissatisfaction that led to disconnection of pay service, HBO developed the "Midas Touch" Incentive Program. HBO's Customer Service Representative Training Program teaches service representatives certain techniques to locate and hopefully remove the source of a customer's dissatisfaction. HBO used a "mystery caller" program to motivate the representatives to use the techniques they had been taught. If the representative used these techniques when a mystery caller phoned, he or she would then be entitled to a gift of their choice from a catalog. To make the program even more exciting, HBO arranged for each representative to receive two mystery calls, thereby giving them two chances to win.

GENERATING CUSTOMER INVOLVEMENT AND BUILDING SALES

Contests are a particularly useful means of eliciting customer response and encouraging involvement. Remember that in a contest the element of chance is replaced by skill; therefore, we can require purchase. The contest must be a valid test of skill; lucky guesses just don't fit in this kind of promotion. Contests of skill run the gamut from creating essays, poems, and rhymes to solving puzzles. The criteria for any kind of contest must be very specific. For a creative entry this may include originality or humor, while for a recipe, ease of preparation and cost are possible criteria for judging.

Several years ago, Ventura Associates ran an extremely interesting and innovative book promotion that literally started a whole new industry. *Who Killed the Robins Family* is a murder mystery with an interesting twist. The reader had the opportunity to solve the crime using clues from the novel. Entrants were asked to answer five specific questions: (1) Who was the murder victim? (2) Who was the killer? (3) Where did the murder take place? (4) How was the victim killed? (5) Why was the victim

ILLUSTRATION 21 *Who Killed the Robins Family* Book Cover

Because *Who Killed the Robins Family* was a contest of skill where we would end up with only one winner, answers to the contest's questions had to be graded by a variety of criteria to ensure we would eventually arrive at just one winner.

Courtesy of William Morrow & Co.

killed? To answer these questions the reader had to read the book very carefully and use sharp deductive reasoning (see Illustration 21). The rules for the contest were clearly stated, as is our practice with any type of promotion, and they carefully outlined how the answers would be evaluated. The winner of the contest won $10,000!

This book was such a hit that the authors recently wrote *The Revenge of the Robins Family,* which has become a *New York Times* best seller!

However, there are some things that prize promotions *cannot* accomplish:

- Prize promotion cannot build brand loyalty for a long-term consumer-sustained franchise.
- In general, prize promotion cannot build an image for a product or a service. The only thing that builds an image is advertising. However, overall image problems can be addressed with prize promotion if it is used as a tool within the total marketing mix. In rare cases, prize promotion alone can help in building an image, but it is a short-term device that cannot dramatically change the general image of a product.
- Prize promotion cannot compensate for inadequate levels of advertising. Unless the general level of advertising and marketing spending is in keeping with the marketplace, it will not enable an advertiser to truly build any long-term effect. For example, a product with a western theme that features a sweepstakes with trips to a dude ranch will help *support* a basic advertising theme. But it would be asking too much to expect a sweepstakes to build this brand image.
- Occasionally, the wider concept of promotion is an effective solution to specific problems. For example, if mass trial is a problem, sampling is a much more efficient device than prize promotions. Prize promotions may have a place as an overlay to a sampling device, but they should not take the place of large-scale mass sampling.

CHAPTER FIVE

Guidelines for Planning Prize Promotions

There are 10 basic steps in planning a prize promotion. They will assure the marketer of maximum benefits.

DETERMINE THE OBJECTIVE

We have already determined that there are a multitude of specific objectives that can be met with prize promotions, but what, specifically, are we attempting to accomplish with this marketing device? The type of offer we create to increase coupon redemption is very different from one used to increase subscription sales. Likewise, if our objective is to increase readership, we would meet it in a different way than increasing response to a questionnaire. So, by establishing the objective, we determine the type of offer we want to make and the most effective way of planning the prize promotion.

CREATE THE APPROPRIATE PROMOTION DEVICE

Here we establish the mechanics of the offer. Should it be a contest, a random drawing, a lucky number, or a matching program? Do we want to create a game offer? Should the entry mechanics involve a cents-off coupon? It is essential to select the right device in the early stages of planning the promotion. The thrust of the prize promotion is obviously different for a contest than for a lucky number offer.

DECIDE ON A THEME

The themes that seem to work best are those that imply luck and the chance to win a dream, and that tie together all the elements of an offer. An anniversary theme is always an interesting idea.

For example, a 25th anniversary celebration can be creatively highlighted by offering prizes related in some way to the number 25; i.e., 25 silver ingots (very appropriate since it also ties in with the traditional 25th silver anniversary). The theme of the offer can also tie in with the benefit of the products. This type of presentation works very well.

Bayer Aspirin ran an offer with a sweepstakes overlay to a cents-off coupon ad. Using three coupons in the ad, they offered three prizes in each prize category. They dubbed the offer the Bayer "Three-For-All" Sweepstakes. The theme tied everything together and made for a very successful prize promotion (see Illustration 22).

ESTABLISH A BUDGET

In creating a budget for any prize promotion, there are four primary areas to consider: prizes, administration, collateral material, and advertising.

Prizes

Chapter Six is an extensive discussion of the development of prize structures. Unfortunately, there is no formula that can specify precisely the number of entries you will receive for each dollar you put into a offer. However, the answers to two basic questions can give you a guideline for determining your prize budget:

1. What is your estimate of the increase in sales that will result from the prize promotion? If you can gauge the effect your promotion will have on future sales, you can determine how much the offer is worth to you.
2. What kind of prize promotion and prizes are being offered by your competition? Your prizes should be equal in value or more enticing than your competitors'.

You should not try to promote a multimagazine subscription business with a prize budget of only $50,000 if all the major players in that field are spending multimillions on prizes. On the other hand, a vitamin company can easily mount a prize promotion with a prize budget under $20,000 because competitors in this field generally offer smaller prizes.

ILLUSTRATION 22 The Bayer $100,000 Three-For-All Sweepstakes

The Three-For-All theme of this promotion tied together the three coupons for different Bayer products and prize choices in each major prize level.

THE BAYER $100,000 "THREE-FOR-ALL" SWEEPSTAKES

GRAND PRIZE

Choose one of three new Chevrolets!

A luxurious Caprice Classic Wagon, a sporty Camaro, or a front-wheel drive Celebrity. An exciting 1984 Chevrolet may await you!

FIRST PRIZE

Choose one of three Baron & Hennessy mink coats!

Each one is full-length and superbly designed. And you get to pick the coat that makes you look your absolute best!

OVER 8000 OTHER PRIZES

25 SECOND PRIZES

Three piece luggage ensemble from Pierre Cardin's "Le Mark XV" collection.

500 THIRD PRIZES

Three colorful designer scarves in luxurious pure silk.

7500 FOURTH PRIZES

Three volume reference library packed with household hints.

HOW TO ENTER—HOW TO WIN

NO PURCHASE NECESSARY

It's easy. You can fill out one or more of the coupons below and use them the next time you buy Bayer, or you can enter by mail (see official rules for details.) Each time you use a coupon, your name will be automatically entered in the sweepstakes. And by using the cents-off coupons, you'll be saving money, too. Hurry! To be eligible for the sweepstakes get your coupons in by April 30, 1984.

OFFICIAL RULES

1. To enter the sweepstakes, fill in the cents-off coupons on this page and redeem them by 4/30/84. Each coupon is a separate entry. When your coupons are returned by your retailer to the clearing house by 6/30/84 you are automatically entered in the sweepstakes.
2. **NO PURCHASE NECESSARY.** You may also enter by printing your name, address and zip code on a 3" x 5" piece of paper and sending it along with the words "Bayer Aspirin" printed on a separate 3" x 5" piece of paper to: Bayer $100,000 "Three-For-All", P.O. Box 551, Lowell, Indiana 46356. Enter as often as you wish, but each entry must be mailed separately. Mailed entries must be received by 4/30/84.
3. Random drawings are under the supervision of VENTURA ASSOCIATES, INC., an independent judging organization whose decisions are final. All prizes will be awarded. One prize per family. Prizes are not transferable and no substitution will be made on any prize except as required by availability.
4. Sweepstakes open to residents of the United States, 18 years of age or older. Employees and their families of Sterling Drug, Inc., and their affiliated companies, their advertising and promotion agencies and VENTURA ASSOCIATES, INC. are not eligible. All federal, state and local laws and regulations apply. Taxes are the responsibility of winners. Void where prohibited or restricted by law. Odds of winning are determined by the total number of entries received. Not responsible for lost, misdirected or late mail or retailer submissions.
5. All winners will be notified by mail. Winners of major prizes will be obligated to sign and return an Affidavit of Eligibility within twenty-one days of date on notification, and winners agree to the use of their name and likeness for publicity purposes. If this Affidavit is not received within the twenty-one day period, alternate winners will be selected at random.

To receive a list of major prize winners, send a stamped, self-addressed envelope to:
"THREE-FOR-ALL" WINNERS LIST
P.O. Box 768, Lowell, IN 46356

The prizes you want, the relief you need, only from Bayer.

BAYER $100,000 "THREE-FOR-ALL" ENTRY FORM

Name________
Address________
City________
State________ Zip____

To be eligible use coupon by 4/30/84.

0444

BAYER $100,000 "THREE-FOR-ALL" ENTRY FORM

Name________
Address________
City________
State________ Zip____

To be eligible use coupon by 4/30/84.

0445

BAYER $100,000 "THREE-FOR-ALL" ENTRY FORM

Name________
Address________
City________
State________ Zip____

To be eligible use coupon by 4/30/84.

0443

Courtesy of Glenbrook Laboratories, Division of Sterling Drug, Inc.

Administration

Administrative costs are usually about $5,000. Of course, this figure depends on the complexity of the offer and any extra costs that are incurred. In Appendix A we take a look at the administrative fees and expenses typically charged by independent judging firms.

In comparing the administrative costs of different sales promotion firms, you need to understand exactly which services are included and which are not. For example, some firms charge low fees, or no administrative fee at all, because they require the sponsor to buy the prizes or the printing from them, and this is the source of the marketing firm's profit. Other firms charge high administrative fees and provide prizes or printing at minimal or no markup.

Collateral Materials

Collateral material is an important part of a prize promotion simply because merchandisers use prize-related materials more often than any other collateral display. Many marketers, dismayed that their costly collateral material has been discarded without being displayed, are delighted to find that virtually every type of business uses prize offer collateral materials.

Obviously, in situations where the sponsor controls the outlets, such as fast-food chains, the collateral material is of great importance because it will be part of the traffic building element we are trying to create (see Illustration 23). Chapter Seven examines various kinds of collateral material, key elements of this material, and the creative process involved.

Advertising

The advertising budget, which is usually the largest single cost in the prize promotion, is determined by the advertising strategy for the product. Advertisers frequently ask prize promotion experts where they should advertise their offer. Our answer, invariably, is to advertise where your customer is. Obviously, you can

ILLUSTRATION 23 Super Bowl XX, Louis Rich Football Sweepstakes Display

Attractive display material that will get up and stay up was the objective of this promotion conducted at deli counters.

Grand Prize:
A Trip for Two to Super Bowl XX!
The winner and a guest will attend Super Bowl XX courtesy of Louis Rich. This grand prize includes transportation, food, lodging and two tickets to the football game of the year.
Win a Trip to Super Bowl XX in the Louis Rich FOOTBALL SWEEPSTAKES
40 First Prizes:
A tailgate party and two tickets to a final NFL home game of the season.
The winners and their guests will attend a final NFL home game of the season. Plus, to end the season right, Louis Rich and a local participating deli will put on a special tailgate party before the game for the winner and their guest!
80 Second Prizes:
Deluxe tailgate picnic basket.
Winners will receive a special Louis Rich Sweepstakes tailgate picnic basket packed with the deli treats it takes to make that next football game unforgettable.
Louis Rich
100 Third Prizes:
NFL history books.
This hardbound collector's edition, 25 Years—The NFL Since 1960, is filled with facts and figures about the teams and players who have made NFL history.
1,000 Fourth Prizes:
Turkey recipe books.
The Year-Round Turkey Cookbook contains hundreds of tasty recipes . . . all featuring the great taste of Louis Rich turkey products.
Over 1,000 Prizes • Enter Today • No Purchase Required • Hurry, Contest Ends November 7, 1985!

Courtesy of Oscar Mayer.

get a higher number of entries if you advertise your sweepstakes in *Lottery News* because you will reach highly responsive people—people who respond to any and all prize promotions. However, if you are selling chickens, your medium is *Poultry Tribune*. That's what chicken buyers read.

In direct mail campaigns the thinking is similar. For example, if you have a magazine offer that has never been successful for the American Family Publishers' mailing list, the use of a sweepstakes can make that list effective. Regardless of the medium you use, a sweepstakes can enhance response and increase your audience.

ESTABLISH APPROPRIATE PRIZES

After establishing a budget, you can now determine the kind of prizes that will result in maximum consumer involvement. Obviously, with a quarter of a million dollars to spend, you can develop a much more exciting prize structure than you can with $25,000. However, you *can* create a successful offer with a small budget. Various techniques for developing a prize structure that will appeal to the specific psychographics and demographics of your audience are discussed in Chapter Six.

WRITE THE RULES

Rules provide the basic conditions governing your offer. This is where you should consult an expert in prize promotion. The most important caveat is that the rules must be written clearly, concisely, and in conformance with the law. Rules are written primarily for the sponsor's protection. Whenever you give an entrant an opportunity to challenge the rules, you loose that protection.

Using rules from another marketer's prize promotion can be an invitation to disaster. Just because a prominent packaged goods company and its leading independent judging organization wrote the rules for a successful, trouble-free prize promotion, you shouldn't assume that the same rules, or even elements of those rules, are right for you. Laws may have changed since their promotion. In addition, your prize promotion will, without a doubt, be at least marginally different from theirs (see Illustrations 24a and 24b).

DESIGN COLLATERAL MATERIAL

We have already discussed the opportunity that prize-related collateral material presents. However, unlike traditional point-

ILLUSTRATION 24a Acme Co. Super Duper Sweepstakes Official Rules

These official rules for the Acme Co. Super Duper Sweepstakes appear complete, but are they?

ACME CO.
SUPER DUPER SWEEPSTAKES

OFFICIAL RULES

Complete the subscription/entry form per instructions and return it in the envelope. All entries must be received by April 30, 1986. Alternative methods of entry may be provided at various times during this sweepstakes.

Sweepstakes open to residents of the United States 18 years of age or under. Employees and their families of Acme Co., their affiliated companies, their advertising, promotion, print, and production agencies and the independent judging organization are not eligible. Void where prohibited by law.

Winners will be determined in random drawings under the supervision of an independent judging organization. One early bird winner will be selected from all entries received by the date indicated elsewhere in the offer.

Winners will be notified by mail and may be asked to sign a statement of eligibility. All federal, state, and local laws and regulations apply. Taxes are the responsibility of winners. Odds of winning are determined by the total number of entries received.

The Super Duper Sweepstakes may be presented in different creative presentations. Winners will have choice of any prize offered at level won. Prizes won by minors may be awarded to parent or legal guardian.

For a list of major prize winners, send a stamped, self-addressed envelope to: Winners List, P.O. Box 765, Hometown, USA 12345.

ILLUSTRATION 24b Elements Missing from the Acme Co. Official Rules

These elements should have been included in order to make the rules foolproof.

The Official Rules for Acme Co. Super Duper Sweepstakes do not state:

1. "No purchase required." Remember, you can't require a purchase, and you must tell the consumer this.
2. "To whom this offer is made available." This would better define our market, ensuring a higher quality of response.
3. "Whose decisions are final." This should be mentioned to avoid any future complications.
4. A time limit by which winners must respond. A company cannot be expected to wait indefinitely to hear from its winners.
5. "No substitution of prize other than as may be necessary due to availability." A winner may want to claim the cash value of a prize, which many companies either may not want or be able to do. Also, if prize merchandise is no longer available, due to the long lead time of some sweepstakes, it is important for a company to leave itself the room for substitution of prizes.

---

of-purchase material, there is a specific formula for creating sweepstakes collateral. What brings people into a store or restaurant is the possibility of a big win. The chance to win a dream is the grabber in this kind of collateral material. That's why the word "WIN!" should appear in large letters. The featured prize should be prominently portrayed, for instance: "Win a Trip on the Orient Express!" or "Win $100,000.00 in Gold!" The number of chances to win should be stated: "Over Five Thousand Chances to Win!" And, of course, don't forget the sponsor! Use the sponsor's logo or the theme of the sponsor's ad campaign. In Revlon's CHAZ "Dream Machine" Sweepstakes, a poster not only assured dominance at point of sale but was the key instrument in determining a winning number. Ads carried inserts with a scratch-off spot revealing the license plate number. To find out

ILLUSTRATION 25 CHAZ "Dream Machine" $1,000,000 Sweepstakes Display Poster

A point-of-sale piece containing winning numbers must be displayed so that customers can match their numbers to it. It can also be used to direct traffic to specific store locations.

if their plate number was a winning number, consumers merely had to check the store display. This technique dramatically increased retailers' use of the display (see Illustration 25).

In addition, it is important that all collateral material include the following statements: (1) "Void where prohibited," (2) "No purchase required," and (3) "Complete rules available." These statements give you protection from liability even if a store revises your material without your knowledge and consent.

Recently, a major manufacturer distributed collateral material without these disclaimers. To make matters worse, store managers wrote the words *Buy* and *Win* on the material, and they used the white space to display the price of the product. However, if the manufacturer had included the disclaimer on the collateral material, even though the store had obscured it, the manufacturer's intent to comply with the law would have protected him.

DETERMINE THE MEDIA

In our discussion of establishing a budget, we outlined the requirements for selecting the appropriate media. Keep in mind that determination of media must be accomplished in the early planning stages of your prize promotion.

IDENTIFY EXTRA PROMOTION OPPORTUNITIES

Look for extra promotional opportunities that may exist in the sweepstakes plan. Could there be a trade overlay in which store managers are offered a chance in their own special sweepstakes? Should there be a sales force incentive overlay?

Since sweepstakes are not everyday events, a special method of communication must be designed so the sales force will be able to explain the event effectively and enthusiastically (see Illustrations 26a and 26b).

THE SUMMIT MEETING

A successful sweepstakes is a complicated undertaking requiring detailed planning and careful coordination of all the participants. It is essential that you meet with the independent judging organization, the sponsor, the advertising agency, sales management, the distributor, and the retailer to develop a precise timetable and assign the responsibilities of each group. A prepromotion meeting plan and critical path analysis should be developed and include all the key operating elements from start to finish.

ILLUSTRATION 26a Cash-in on Avis Sweepstakes Announcement and Entry Form

Promotion dollars can often be spent more effectively on the trade than by stretching them too thin by going to the consumer. This promotion was directed exclusively to travel agents.

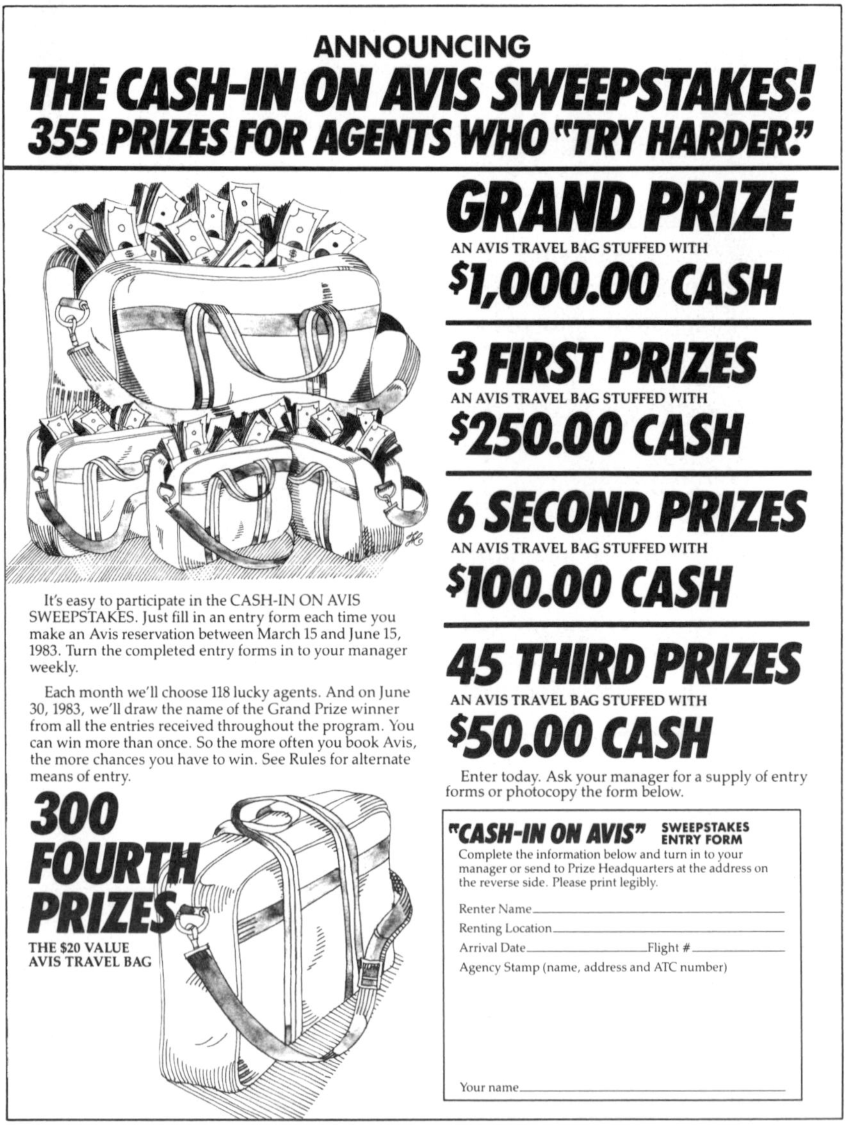

ANNOUNCING
THE CASH-IN ON AVIS SWEEPSTAKES!
355 PRIZES FOR AGENTS WHO "TRY HARDER."
GRAND PRIZE
AN AVIS TRAVEL BAG STUFFED WITH
$1,000.00 CASH
3 FIRST PRIZES
AN AVIS TRAVEL BAG STUFFED WITH
$250.00 CASH
6 SECOND PRIZES
AN AVIS TRAVEL BAG STUFFED WITH
$100.00 CASH
45 THIRD PRIZES
AN AVIS TRAVEL BAG STUFFED WITH
$50.00 CASH
It's easy to participate in the CASH-IN ON AVIS SWEEPSTAKES. Just fill in an entry form each time you make an Avis reservation between March 15 and June 15, 1983. Turn the completed entry forms in to your manager weekly.
Each month we'll choose 118 lucky agents. And on June 30, 1983, we'll draw the name of the Grand Prize winner from all the entries received throughout the program. You can win more than once. So the more often you book Avis, the more chances you have to win. See Rules for alternate means of entry.
300 FOURTH PRIZES
THE $20 VALUE AVIS TRAVEL BAG
Enter today. Ask your manager for a supply of entry forms or photocopy the form below.
"CASH-IN ON AVIS" SWEEPSTAKES ENTRY FORM
Complete the information below and turn in to your manager or send to Prize Headquarters at the address on the reverse side. Please print legibly.
Renter Name
Renting Location
Arrival Date
Flight #
Agency Stamp (name, address and ATC number)
Your name

Courtesy of Avis.

ILLUSTRATION 26b Chock full o'Nuts $1,000,000.00 Golden Scoopstakes Trade Sheet

The trade promotion was developed in this "Deal Sheet." This promotion not only sold in but sold through as well.

Courtesy of Chock full o'Nuts Corporation.

This is an important process that will enable you to ensure that all deadlines can be met and specific assignments of each element of the promotion can be fulfilled. A few of the important points in this critical path are the dates for the development of a contract, rules and prize structure, arrangements for the availability of entries, performing the drawing, preparing potential winners lists, the signing of affidavits, preparation of drafts of notification, ordering prizes, and the release of bonds.

An independent judging organization should be involved from the very beginning because it brings to the promotion the single most important component—EXPERIENCE. Many companies try to handle a sweepstakes internally. This is like trying to build a house after watching a professional build one. Not only is it inefficient but it can be dangerous.

The role of the independent judging organization involves more than merely writing a set of rules and picking a lucky number out of a hat. You must be able to rely on them for support and involvement in every facet of your prize promotion. If you choose the right judging firm, you will gain a valuable marketing consultant who will take your prize promotion all the way from its development through its implementation. The firm will be involved in every issue—not limited to just what they've outlined in their standard proposal letter. It will be involved in reviewing all creative presentations, as well as in discussing ideas that you may have. Most important, it will be available to you as needed to contribute ideas and solve problems.

For more elaborate offers it is sometimes desirable to call in additional outside consultants at the very outset of planning. Depending on the program, you may wish to consult media buyers, accounting firms, computer specialists, or packaging experts, to name a few. In addition, you may find it useful to get the perspective of people in your company who are not directly involved in marketing.

While planning a prize promotion may look quite complicated to someone on the outside, it is just routine to the experienced practitioner. This elaborate step-by-step plan should not be threatening to a sweepstakes client. It should, however, make you fully aware of the levels of professionalism and skill that are required in running a successful prize promotion.

Upon the completion of the sweepstakes, the same kind of skill and planning will be necessary. It may seem as if the only postpromotion job is the simple matter of doing the drawing. Don't be deceived. The tasks are many, and they require the special expertise that only a sales promotion firm can provide. They include everything from preparing lists of potential major prize winners, looking for postpromotion opportunities, creating affidavits, and obtaining client approval on drafts of notification, right down to notification of the winners and awarding of the prizes.

CHAPTER SIX

Creating a Prize Structure

The chance to win a valuable prize is the engine that propels a prize promotion. The more attractive the prize seems, the more likely someone is to participate in a prize promotion. There are other factors that will influence participation, including probability of winning, aesthetic appeal of the graphics, and how the offer is stated. But it is clearly the prize structure that is a key element in the success or failure of any prize promotion.

The most compelling, appealing sweepstakes will receive few entries if the prizes don't appeal to the audience the offer is directed to. This is one of the reasons that sweepstakes have not been testable as a marketing concept. Because we need to have a prize of sufficient value to influence participation, we cannot test a sweepstakes in one market region with a smaller prize and use the results of the test to project the prize offer's success in other market regions (see Illustration 27).

Focus groups confirm what experience has indicated: the best prize structures are those with a large first prize—a "dream" prize—and a large number of lower level prizes. This allows the marketer to use a copy line such as "Over One Thousand Chances to Win!" Making the chance of winning seem a probability rather than a possibility undoubtedly draws a greater response (see Illustrations 28 and 29).

While there must be some middle-level prizes, keep in mind that their importance is minimal. In actual market tests, there was actually less participation in an offer with a Grand Prize of $100,000 than there was in an offer with a Grand Prize of $25,000 and thousands of chances to win an item of considerably less value.

Money is not a particularly compelling prize unless it is a "dream" amount. So cash prizes of less than $25,000 won't have the appeal that merchandise worth a comparable amount will have. That is, we can take $10,000 and merchandise it into a fabulous vacation, a car, even gold or mink coats, and receive much more interest and participation than with a cash prize of $10,000.

This is especially true with prizes of even smaller amounts. Winnings of $5, $10, $25, and $50 in cash can be used to pay bills and therefore are not the least exciting. On the other hand, the same amounts can be used to create items of interest, such as jewelry and cameras—things people desire but are not likely to buy for themselves.

ILLUSTRATION 27 Shillcraft Super Sweepstakes Brochure

Early Bird prizes create a sense of urgency for those receiving a sweepstakes offer early in the mailing schedule, long before the sweepstakes expiration date is near.

Courtesy of Shillcraft.

Cash itself as a first prize will create more entries as dollar amounts increase. The most obvious example is state lotteries where participants can win prizes in excess of $20 million. Even though the chance of winning a $20 million lottery is infinitesimal, these big money prizes attract enough people to create ticket lines that stretch around the block.

We see similar excitement generated by big money prizes in sweepstakes. An excellent example is American Family Publishers' $10 million offer. When compared to prize promotions by other magazine companies whose prizes are considerably less, we can see by the number of responses that the American Family

ILLUSTRATION 28 American Family Publishers Ten Million Dollar Sweepstakes

Even in huge amounts, it is often better to promote money prizes in terms of what dollars can buy. This stimulates consumers' imaginations adding even greater dramatic impact to your offer.

Courtesy of American Family Publishers.

ILLUSTRATION 29 Revlon's Look Like a Million, Live Like a Millionaire Announcement of $1,000,000 Grand Prize

Revlon justified their enormous $1,000,000 Grand Prize based on the fact that sweepstakes participants either had to visit retailers or write for an entry blank.

Publishers offer generates a lot more excitement. However, don't infer from this that prize promotion can be employed only when you give away enormous amounts of money; half of all the prize offers have budgets of less than $20,000.

There are a number of techniques that can make small amounts of money look larger. Offering a choice of prizes creates excitement and does not add to the cost. For example, if in one program we offered an Oldsmobile as the Grand Prize, we would not get the same participation as we would in another in which we offer the Grand Prize winner a choice of an Oldsmobile, a Pontiac, a Chevrolet, a trip to Europe, or $10,000 worth of diamonds and gold. And, interestingly, the cost to the marketer is identical. In both programs we are still giving away a single prize, but in the second we are able to portray an enticing array of prizes and create the fantasy factor that we are looking for (see Illustration 30).

In addition, $20,000 can be a meaningful budget figure because prize promotion experts can buy merchandise at or below wholesale. A really effective marketing consulting firm can buy merchandise at a fraction of its cost. Sometimes we can trade advertising exposure for the prize itself. We can barter free trips or cars in exchange for featuring the airline or the automotive company in our advertising. The manufacturer's logo and slogan are used in significant circulation in exchange for their merchandise to be used as prizes. All television game shows work on this principle.

In developing a prize structure, an effective marketer will therefore focus on the Grand Prize and the low-end prizes. The goal is to create a pyramidal prize structure with a Grand Prize at the top, several middle-level prizes, and a large number of low-end prizes. Although, as noted, the Grand Prize must be of dream quality, the low-end prizes—those at the bottom of the prize structure—must have a high *perceived* value, while actually costing the marketer no more than a few dollars.

It is also important to take into account the cost of shipping. More than one disappointed sweepstakes operator offered 25,000 low-end prizes and found that the cost of shipping them was greater than the cost of the prizes themselves. For example, a fast-food operator who was excited by the prospect of offering a mug emblazoned with his logo was dismayed to find that the

ILLUSTRATION 30 Great American Magazines, Inc., Great American Dream Sweepstakes, Prize Brochure

This prize schedule shows how prize choice can expand the apparency of value. Note too that the 50,000 sets of books added $600,000 of retail value at a fraction of the cost.

Courtesy of Great American Magazines, Inc.

75-cent mug cost $1.25 to ship and that he could expect a significant amount of breakage, resulting in many disappointed customers.

Similar difficulties arise with prizes like T-shirts where size is a factor, necessitating correspondence with winners to ascertain their choice of size. The all-important bottom-end prize should be something that can be inexpensively shipped at bulk rate with a notification of winning right inside, thereby lowering shipping and handling costs. However, you must keep in mind that the prize you choose must have universal appeal.

Typically successful low-end prizes are jewelry, tote bags, scarves, paperback and hardcover books, and printed items of all descriptions, such as note paper or greeting cards. All of these items meet the criteria of having general mass appeal, a cost of no more than 25 percent of the retail price, and the ability to be mailed under the bulk rate postage requirements, which are a fraction of UPS costs.

The development of a prize structure really starts with identifying the group you hope to reach—obviously, mink coats are not the perfect prize for Friends of the Animals. However, prize structure development goes much deeper than that. Specifically, it addresses the question: What kind of prizes will motivate the kind of people we want to appeal to?

Sometimes the prize itself can be a self-selector of participation. That is, someone selling land sites in Arizona who wants to limit participation to those specifically interested in this land might give away one of his own sites in a prize promotion. Therefore, a person not wanting land would not enter. Generally, however, it is bad psychology to give away something you manufacture as a prize. The reason is simply that consumers will sometimes postpone a purchase to see if they've won the item. Obviously, we don't want anything to inhibit a purchase.

The perfect prize structure starts with an understanding of the psychographics and demographics of the group you want to reach. Is the audience upscale or downscale? Older or younger? Upper or lower income? However, there are some general rules that transcend the background of the participants.

These rules are often surprising because they contradict what is assumed to be marketing common sense. For example, celebrity prizes are invariably a disappointment. Such sweepstakes prizes as "Lunch with Jerry Lewis" are nearly always a disappointment—not because Jerry Lewis is not scintillating but because most people are intimidated by celebrities.

Frequently, marketers who want to appeal to teenagers believe there is nothing more compelling than winning a date with a rock star. One of these programs, run recently by a recording company, produced less than a hundred entries, even though it was nationally advertised. While teenage girls love to scream and fantasize about a particular star, the thought of spending an evening with him was so threatening and intimidating that they wouldn't even fill out an entry blank!

To make a prize promotion interesting and exciting, you want to make the dollar amounts appear as large as possible. This can sometimes be accomplished through insurance funding or by a payout over a number of years. For example, a million-dollar prize need not cost the marketer anywhere near $1 million. Paid out at $50,000 a year for 20 years, the prize can be financed by a single-pay annuity. Then, depending on the age of the winner, it could cost significantly less than $1 million. Another option for financing money prizes is through the use of a bond in which the interest is paid to the winner with the bond reverting to the company after 20 years. Depending on its accounting situation, a company might be able to carry that $1 million on the books as an asset and therefore not charge the marketing cost of that million dollar prize at all.

Prizes that are awarded utilizing insurance are directly related to the magic of compound interest. Take, for example, a most successful offer: "Win Retirement." The rules stipulated that a person would receive the prize at age 65. The sweepstakes was open to individuals 55 years of age and younger. The prize of $1 million on retirement was to be paid out at age 65 at $100,000 a year for 10 years. The actual maximum cost of that prize was less than $150,000. As a matter of fact, had the winner been young enough, the cost to the marketer would have been less than $50,000. The maximum of $150,000 assumed a 55-year-old winner and took into account the fact that the insurance company didn't have to pay out any money for 10 years and therefore had the use of the $150,000 for those 10 years. Furthermore, the total amount of money wasn't actually paid out for another 10 years. Also, if the winner had died anytime between the date of the winning and reaching the age of 65, the insurance company had no cost at all.

The potential of insurance and annuity prizes transcends cash. For example, one of the most successful prizes ever, as measured by actual number of entries and focus group reaction, was part of a recent cruise line program where the prize was "A New Car Every Year for Life." The offer was the American dream—driving a brand-new car every year—conjuring up an image of a tremendous number of cars.

In actuality, the rules disclosed that the winners would receive a new car each year of their life through a car leasing plan, upon presentation of a copy of their current drivers' license and the return of last year's car. The winner did not receive a $10,000 car every year but simply the value of a one-year lease. The *actual* cost of this prize, depending on the winner's age, was considerably less than the *perceived* value.

The purpose of this type of prize development is to keep costs within an affordable range, not to dupe the participants. It is vital to fully disclose the terms and conditions of the offer. Obviously, a marketer who does not disclose the limitations of an offer in a manner that can be understood by a reasonably intelligent person would be liable under regulations governing deceptive advertising. The marketer is also required to disclose in the rules that the prize is nontransferable and will not be awarded unless the winner meets the terms spelled out in the official rules.

However, we can disclose all the limitations to the offer and still present an exciting prize within an affordable range. Currently, Ventura Associates is conducting an offer that promises free vacations for life. A two-week annual vacation is an important part of most workers' lives. The rules clearly state that the prize is a vacation of up to two weeks each year, taken at one time or spread over the year. An exciting feature of this prize is that the maximum value of $2,500 per vacation exceeds the U.S. Department of Commerce estimate of what the average American family spends annually on vacations. In addition, most consumers would not use the entire $2,500, and the prize can be funded with less than $20,000 through the purchase of an annuity.

The American Express "Fly Free for Life" prize promotion, in which the winner received unlimited flight privileges for life, is one of the most famous programs ever run. Yet, this successful prize promotion was accomplished at a very low cost because after the first year, the novelty and excitement of constant travel wore off rather quickly. In addition, for most people, the responsibilities of job and family did not allow them to simply pick up and leave whenever they wanted to. Furthermore, the prize was strictly air travel for one; the winner was responsible for the cost of his companion's fare, plus accommodations and meals. Obviously, there is the marketing risk that the prize would be won by someone who travels for a living, but in cases like this you must compare the possible liability with the guaranteed promotability of the program.

As we have shown, fulfilling the fantasies of a particular group of individuals is often considerably less expensive than you might imagine. A prize consisting of a golfing vacation at La Costa in California, which might be used for a golf organization membership promotion, would have much greater appeal to hard-core golfers than a two-week vacation in Europe, yet the cost would be significantly less (see Illustration 31).

In summary, when the goal is to appeal to a narrow audience, the prizes should be related to the particular interests of that group. In addition, interesting and exciting prizes can be offered at minimal cost to the marketer.

An essential factor to consider when planning your prize structure is that the average American family's estimated disposable income is $22,694.[1] Therefore, although a prize of a television set seems hardly the stuff that dreams are made of, a large percentage of the population will drive miles to patronize a particular store simply for the chance of winning one.

As in all marketing decisions, it is a mistake to equate your preferences with those of your potential audience. You may want to win an African safari, or a rafting trip on the Amazon, or even a climbing expedition in the Himalayas, but it is doubtful that any of these will be attractive to the general public. In a recent survey, sweepstakes entrants were asked to check the trip they would most like to win:

A trip for two to any three cities in Europe.
A trip for two to any three cities in the United States.
A trip for two around the world.
A trip for four to Disneyland/Disney World.

[1]U.S. Department of Commerce, Bureau of the Census, estimated after-tax income.

ILLUSTRATION 31 USGA Golfer's Dream Sweepstakes

As the United States Golf Association proves, the more you know about your prospects, the better you can create a prize structure that will appeal to your target audience.

Courtesy of the United States Golf Association.

Over 50 percent of the respondents chose the trip to Disneyland/Disney World. This trip would cost about $5,000. The other trip costs went as high as $25,000. One of the most successful trip prizes we recall offered 30 days on a Greyhound bus. Surprised?

Another interesting psychographic factor is that for prize promotion respondents, regardless of their disposable income, the chance to win a valuable prize—or even a marginally valuable prize—is extremely compelling. In Las Vegas, people with six-figure incomes and more play the 25-cent slot machines and delight in winning $2 or $3. Similarly, many sweepstakes respondents come from upper-income groups. It is simply the opportunity to win a prize—any prize—and even the idea of winning, that creates such tremendous appeal.

Direct marketers first ran "Everybody Wins" sweepstakes in the early 1960s. The prizes were jewelry items with a value of a mere 20 or 30 cents. The original sponsor, Sunset House, received many letters from winners who were delighted because they had never won anything before. In further tracking these customers, Sunset House discovered that by making everyone a winner they had increased their number of long-term, loyal customers.

Sponsors of a sweepstakes should also recognize that in planning a prize promotion they are frequently working 18 months to two years ahead of the general marketplace. That is, a client planning a sweepstakes today may not finalize plans for another year, and prizes may not be awarded for two years. Therefore, the temptation to cash in on present-day fads should be avoided. By including fad items in your prize structure, you run the risk of having prizes with negligible appeal at the time the program finally runs. More than one offer has failed simply because the excitement of the prize, which was enormous at creation, had reached oversaturation at publication. In addition, purchasing an inventory of 1985 cars makes little sense when you won't be awarding prizes until 1987.

The constraint of working two years ahead also requires budgeting considerations. For example, in 1980 silver prices hit bottom, affecting many marketers who regularly used sterling silver as a first or second prize. These marketers found themselves significantly over budget simply because the value of their prizes dropped when silver prizes plummeted. Avoiding this kind of budgeting problem involves more than merely recognizing the effects of inflation. It requires consideration of fluctuations in pricing of such prizes as imported goods, antiques, items in limited supply, or any item that relies on precious materials. When budgeting for prizes like trips (i.e., a trip to anywhere in the continental United States), you should budget for the furthest possible distance that a winner may choose to go.

When budgeting for prizes that rely on the ingenuity or skill of the winner, it is always good practice to budget on the high side. There have been cases in which marketers did not give themselves enough leeway in their budgets. When offering a prize of all the silver dollars that a winner could shovel in five minutes, one marketer borrowed bags full of coins from a local bank and had his employees actually shovel money for five-minute periods. The marketer then based his budget on the results of these trials. An appropriate caution, you may think. But the grand prize winner, when notified that he won, filled his basement with sand, took a month off from work, and actually practiced shoveling for eight hours every day! At the end of the prize promotion, the actual cost to the marketer was two and a half times greater than his projected budget. Not only had the marketer failed to consider that the winner might train for the occasion, but he did not compensate for the fact that an individual shoveling for money he will keep is significantly more motivated.

The ingenuity of consumers who stand to gain financially should never be underestimated; it has often outwitted the unwary marketing planner. More than one winner of all the groceries they can gather in five minutes has convinced an unscrupulous supermarket owner to carefully stock the store with lobster and other expensive items, all of which would be paid for by the sponsor, in an effort to turn his marginal prize into a much larger one. It's important to recognize that with the marketing benefit of a unique prize structure comes the marketing liability of not being able to closely estimate total costs.

In many cases it is not desirable to be overly creative in choosing prizes. Marketers will find that interest in Louis XIV chairs and unusual paintings is significantly lower than interest in cars and television sets. This is apparent when examining the kinds of items most often chosen from an incentive company's prize brochure. A brochure may offer many different prizes, from sewing machines and golf clubs to works of art. Yet, television

ILLUSTRATION 32 C Town Supermarkets Sweepstakes

A powerful headline, such as C Town Supermarkets' "You Can Win a Truckload of Groceries and the Truck!" accompanied by exciting graphics, creates the ultimate dream for customers.

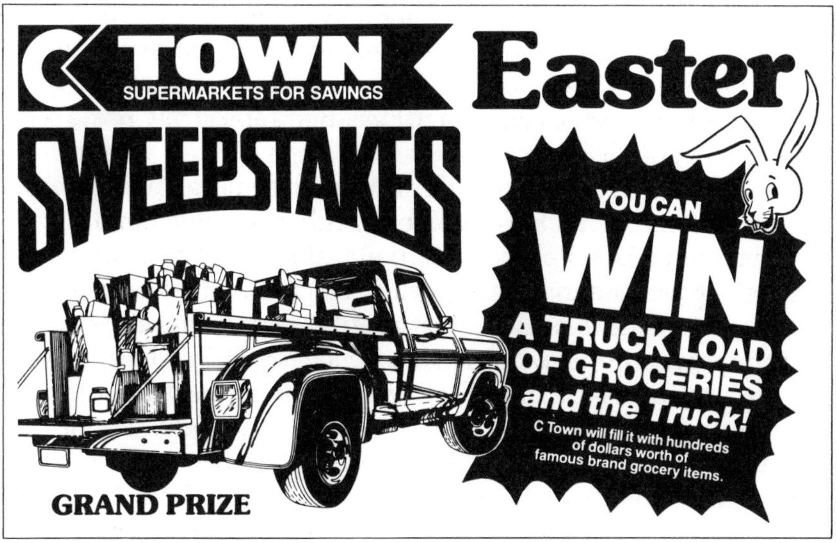

Courtesy of C Town Supermarkets, Krasdale Foods, Inc.

sets are consistently claimed by winners. It appears that an American household cannot have too many TVs.

Because the appeal of a prize depends solely on the tastes of the potential winner and not on that of the sponsor, unique prizes are often not the best choice. Furthermore, prizes that are simple to portray and explain are often preferable because they leave space in advertising material for promoting your product. For example, if your prize is a TV, the words *General Electric 21-Inch Television* say it all, whereas a prize of sophisticated exercise equipment necessitates a rather lengthy description, taking up precious ad space. C Town Supermarkets ran an offer in which the prize structure allowed the use of an interesting visual of a truck overflowing with groceries, and the headline: "You Can Win a Truckload of Groceries and the Truck." No lengthy descriptions were needed here—these few words told the whole story (see Illustration 32).

The offer, of course, must take into account the individuality of each potential entrant. This may seem an impossible task, but if we present an offer of general appeal to the hundreds of thousands or even millions of people we want to reach, we can later negotiate with the final winner on a one-to-one basis. So, for example, while it may be creatively sound to offer a trip around the world as a Grand Prize, the winner may be more interested in six tickets to Disney World. Thus, the marketer must recognize both the unique advantages and disadvantages that come with the awarding of prizes.

Prize promotions for children present unique opportunities as well as some perplexing problems. For one thing, children are easier to excite, and therefore prize promotions that appeal to kids are less expensive to run. They are also easier to influence, and great care must be taken so that they aren't misled. The danger in prize promotions for children lies in the prizes themselves. The prizes must be items that can be easily and carefully explained. Indeed, the entire offer must be clear to the young participants, not only because there are strict business regulations governing advertising for children, but because it is just good business ethics. One successful prize offer for children gave them the chance to "Win Allowance for a Year." The prize was simply a $10 a week allowance for one year. The total cost of the prize was a mere $520.

Since young people are more easily misled, it is the responsibility of a marketer to communicate with them at a level they can understand. If you offer teenage girls the opportunity to have their phone bill paid for a year, it is important to state whether or not this prize includes long-distance calls and telephone installation as well as any other limitations on the offer.

In designing prize structures, marketers must be as astute as any professional buyer of merchandise. But the major difference is that the typical buyer usually deals with a narrow line of merchandise and therefore develops special expertise in that line. The scarf buyer for Sears, for example, may purchase $20 million a year in scarves and can therefore become an expert in every part of the scarf industry. The buyer of prizes, on the other hand, must purchase a wide variety of products—everything from scarves and tote bags to trips.

Although prize buyers cannot always be expected to purchase merchandise at the best possible price, they need to have strong business acumen to avoid serious business mistakes. Because prize buyers are representing a third party—the sponsor—and the merchandise is being distributed in the name of that sponsor, any mistakes tend to be longer lasting and more damaging. If K mart were to mistakenly buy 500 defective telephones, consumers who purchased them could simply return them to K mart, and K mart could either return them to the manufacturer or absorb that loss. Five hundred defective phones shipped to prize winners in the name of a third-party sponsor could seriously damage the reputation of the sponsor.

One incident illustrates this problem at it's extreme. A candy company wanted to create a unique sweepstakes and therefore decided to give away pets as prizes. The prize buyer found a company that sold fish in a plastic bag and was assured that they were capable of being delivered through the mail in cardboard boxes. Before he purchased the fish, the buyer had the good sense to send 50 of them to members of a trade association and ask them to call him collect to report whether the fish had arrived safely. Interestingly, all 50 said that the fish had in fact arrived healthy and that no shipping problems had occurred. Unfortunately, this test was done in April. The actual prizes were shipped in November and sat in boxcars in Chicago. What each of the 5,000 winning children received was a chunk of ice with a goldfish in the center. Obviously, the company is still trying to recoup from the consumer mail problems resulting from that blunder.

CHAPTER SEVEN

Sweepstakes Creative

This chapter introduces the uses of various media for promotional support of your sweepstakes, including television commercials, free-standing inserts, space ads, game cards, hangtags and neckers, and all components of direct mail packages. Now we come to the Basic Formula for sweepstakes creative, and take you through it step by step.

In one respect, sales promotion advertising is the same as other forms of advertising—the creative execution. To the dismay of creative staff, a proven, time-tested Basic Formula works best. Research has shown that when creative approaches are tested against the formula approach, the Basic Formula approach wins every time. For example, if you were to run a cents-off coupon with a creative theme such as "ACME PRODUCT'S INFLATION FIGHTER" versus one that says "SAVE 7¢" or "7¢ OFF," the latter would win hands down. In fact, the Basic Formula approach will get twice the redemption of a more "creative" one.

This precept is no less true for sweepstakes creative. Again, the best approach for a strong sweepstakes presentation is not creative but Basic Formula.

THE BASIC FORMULA FOR SWEEPSTAKES CREATIVE

1. Create Motivation

WIN! It is one of the most powerful words in the English language. Use the word WIN as often as you can, sprinkling it liberally throughout your sweepstakes presentation. Sweepstakes lend themselves to a loud, carnival-type presentation. The headline should *scream* the word *WIN.* And to emphasize it further, enclose it in big, jagged bursts and brightly colored violators and banners (see Illustration 33).

2. Identify the Sponsor

Display the sweepstakes sponsor's name prominently in the presentation. Generally, at the top of your ad, brochure, game ticket, or at the beginning of your broadcast commercial, you should say, "The makers of Bitsy Butters present . . ." or "Play the Acme 'Save 'n Win' Sweepstakes." Note that you should avoid the temptation to state something like, "Play Acme's 'Save 'n Win' Sweepstakes." Here the sponsor's name has been rendered possessive by an apostrophe. Companies generally require that their name stand un-apostrophed for legal reasons and to ensure public recognition.

Obviously, the reason for putting the sponsor's name up front is to ensure that the name and product will be identified with all the wonderful opportunities that are being offered in the sweepstakes. Keep in mind how much the sponsor is spending on his sweepstakes and all the prizes he is offering. You never want to lose sight of your number one goal—selling more product.

ILLUSTRATION 33 *New Woman* On the Go Sweepstakes Entry Renewal Form; Letraset Destination Hawaii Sweepstakes

WIN! is an important word in sweepstakes. In these samples created by Ventura Associates for Letraset and *New Woman* magazine, it is used liberally. In the *New Woman* piece, the word *WIN* is in all four corners. In the Letraset piece, "Win with Letraset" is splashed across the top of the piece.

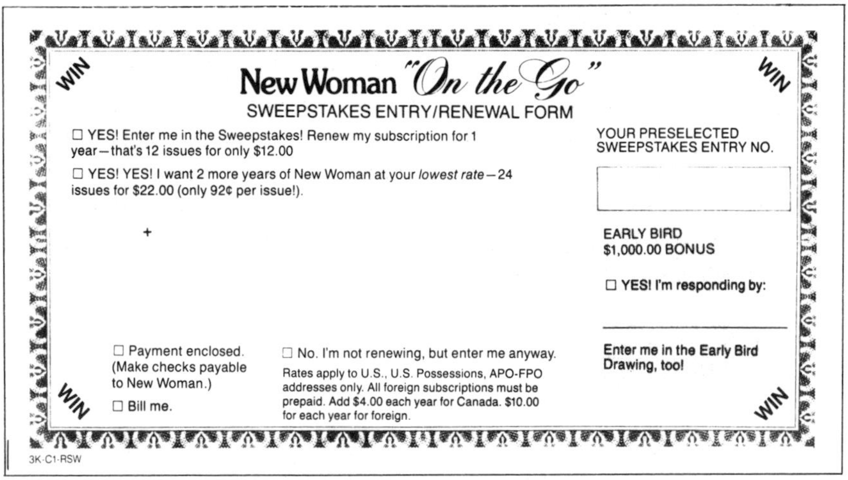
WIN
New Woman "On the Go"
WIN
SWEEPSTAKES ENTRY/RENEWAL FORM

☐ YES! Enter me in the Sweepstakes! Renew my subscription for 1 year—that's 12 issues for only $12.00

☐ YES! YES! I want 2 more years of New Woman at your *lowest rate*—24 issues for $22.00 (only 92¢ per issue!).

YOUR PRESELECTED SWEEPSTAKES ENTRY NO.

EARLY BIRD
$1,000.00 BONUS

☐ YES! I'm responding by:

Enter me in the Early Bird Drawing, too!

☐ Payment enclosed. (Make checks payable to New Woman.)

☐ Bill me.

☐ No. I'm not renewing, but enter me anyway.

Rates apply to U.S., U.S. Possessions, APO-FPO addresses only. All foreign subscriptions must be prepaid. Add $4.00 each year for Canada. $10.00 for each year for foreign.

WIN
WIN

3K-C1-RSW

Courtesy of *New Woman* Magazine.

ILLUSTRATION 33 *(continued)*

Win with Letraset!

. . .FOR GREATER SALES VOLUME!
. . .FOR TERRIFIC PRIZES!

The more you know about the wide range of Letraset products, the easier it will be for you to sell them! Plus, when you answer the questions, complete the entry form and return it by the deadline, you'll have the chance to win the Grand Prize trip for 2 to Hawaii—or any of more than 1,000 prizes in our Grand Prize and Bonus Quarterly Drawings!

LETRAMAX MOUNTING, ILLUSTRATION, AND MECHANICAL BOARDS, FROM LETRASET.

The Letramax artboard line provides a wide variety of surfaces for mounting, illustration and mechanicals, ranging in size from 15" x 20" to 32" x 40". Included are:

The *LETRAMAX 100 MOUNTING BOARD* has a deep black surface and is solid black all the way through—you never have to blacken the edges with a marker! Its toothy texture eliminates distracting sheen and it accepts both wet and dry mounting adhesives.

LETRAMAX 2200 COLD PRESS ILLUSTRATION BOARD offers a medium tooth surface for wet and dry media including gouache, tempera, watercolor, charcoal, pencils and much more. Its rag content provides even absorption of wet media for better control. Its super white surface enhances color intensity and fidelity.

LETRAMAX 1000 ALL PURPOSES HOT PRESS ILLUSTRATION BOARD is designed and priced for high volume mechanical work. Its smooth white surface maintains its original quality even after erasure, tape picking and scraping. Designed for all media used for mechanicals, the surface can be stripped for repositioning sections of art.

LETRAMAX 2000 RULING MECHANICAL BOARD has a smooth, super-white surface that produces crisp line work and clean mechanicals. It is durable and responsive, producing original-quality mechanicals even after reworking.

LETRAMAX 4000 PREMIUM RULING MECHANICAL BOARD possesses a sparkling white surface which sets a new standard for inking and linework. This crisp, bright surface allows for truly impressive sharpness, density and heightened contrast when used for inking. It also offers superior performance with all studio materials including technical pens, airbrush and all types of adhesives. Even after extensive reworking and erasure of ink lines, this premium mechancial board will maintain its original clean, white look.

To enter the Grand Prize Drawing, simply complete the Entry Form at right, answering the questions about Letraset products (answers can all be found in this mailing).

BEAT THE JUNE 30, 1985 DEADLINE FOR EXTRA CHANCES TO WIN IN THE BONUS QUARTERLY DRAWING!!

THE SECOND QUARTERLY BONUS DRAWING

Here's what you could win in our second Bonus Drawing—remember, you've got to beat the 6/30/85 deadline to be eligible to win!

FIRST PRIZE
1 AWARDED—Fisher Complete State-of-the-Art Stereo System

SECOND PRIZE
2 Awarded—Fisher Portable Stereo System

THIRD PRIZE
5 Awarded—SONY FM Stereo Walkman

Your completed and mailed entry form doubles as an entry in both the Grand Prize Drawing and—provided it's received by the deadline—also the Bonus Quarterly Drawing!

OFFICIAL RULES

1. No purchase necessary. Simply complete official entry blank per instructions, hand printing your name, address, and zip code in plain block letters. You may obtain an official entry form by submitting an official "Sign Up" form provided by Letraset USA, or by writing to 1985 Letraset "Destination Hawaii" Entry Form, P.O. Box 621, Lowell, IN 46399.
2. Mail your entry to Letraset "Destination Hawaii", P.O. Box 503, Lowell, Ind. 46399. Only one entry per individual per month. Only official entry forms will be accepted. All entries must be received by December 1, 1985. Not responsible for lost, illegible, misdirected or late mail.
3. Winners will be selected from among all entries received in random drawings conducted by VENTURA ASSOCIATES, INC., an independent judging organization whose decisions are final. By entering this sweepstakes entrants agree to, and accept these rules. Winners will be notified by mail and may be required to sign and return an affidavit of eligibility within 21 days of date on notification. If completed affidavit is not received within 21 days, alternate winner may be selected. Winners agree to use of their names and likenesses without additional compensation.
4. Quarterly drawings, in addition to the grand drawing to be held after December 31, 1985, will be held, and quarterly bonus prizes will be awarded. Winners will be drawn from those official entries submitted during each quarter. Deadlines for quarterly entries are March 31, 1985, June 30, 1985, and September 30, 1985. Winners will be notified in the month following the drawing deadline.
5. Grand Prize Hawaiian vacation includes round-trip air-fare to Hawaii, first class hotel accommodations for two for seven days, plus $500 cash. Travel Prize is subject to space and departure availability and must be taken by Dec. 31, 1986. Three (3) first prizes consist of 19" TV, VCR and video camera. Five (5) second prize winners will receive Vitamaster System I (7000) exercise machine. Ten (10) third prize winners will receive a Structo Portable Gas Grill. One thousand (1,000) fourth prizes of a Letraset Digital Desk Clock will be awarded.
6. This sweepstakes is open to residents of the United States, 18 years of age and older who sell Letraset products, employed by authorized Letraset retail distributors. Void where prohibited by law. All federal, state and local laws and regulations apply. Employees and their families of Letraset USA Inc., its parent, subsidiaries, and affiliates, and their advertising, and promotion agencies and VENTURA ASSOCIATES, INC., are not eligible. No duplicate major prize winners. No substitution for prizes except as necessary due to prize availability. Taxes are the responsibility of the winners. Odds of winning determined by number of eligible entries received.
7. For a list of major prize winners, send a stamped, self-addressed envelope to Letraset "Destination Hawaii" Winners, P.O. Box 727, Lowell, IN 46399.

LETRASET "DESTINATION HAWAII" SWEEPSTAKES

ENTRY FORM

☐ **YES!** Enter me in the Letraset "Destination Hawaii" Sweepstakes: I've answered all of the questions below and completed the form.

☐ **YES!** I've beaten the deadline of June 30, 1985. Enter me in the Bonus Quarterly Drawing, and let me know if I'm a winner! I understand that this Drawing will take place early in July.

1. Letramax Artboards range in size from ______ to ______.
2. Letramax 4000 Premium Ruling Mechanical Board sets a new standard for inking and ______.
3. The high quality surfaces of Letramax Ruling Mechanical Boards retain their original ______ even after reworking.
4. Letramax 2200 Cold Press Illustration Board offers a medium tooth surface for wet and ______ media.

▶ *Name* ______

Retail Store ______

Address ______

City ______ *State* ______ *Zip* ______

Courtesy of Letraset U.S.A.

ILLUSTRATION 33 *(concluded)*

Win with Letraset!

...FOR GREATER SALES VOLUME!

...FOR TERRIFIC PRIZES!

The more you know about the wide range of Letraset products, the easier it will be for you to sell them! Plus, when you answer the questions, complete the entry form and return it by the deadline, you'll have the chance to win the Grand Prize trip for 2 to Hawaii—or any of more than 1,000 prizes in our Grand Prize and Bonus Quarterly Drawings!

LETRASET MASKING FILMS AND OPAQUING MARKERS

Letraset Masking Films and Opaquing Markers include several quality products which are indispensable to the printer's craft. These films and markers are designed for ease and versatility in application in usage, working *with* strippers so they can concentrate on their craft and achieve optimum results easily.

LETRASET'S STRIPPING MATERIALS INCLUDE:
Letrapaque Masking Film • Letramask Film
Letraline Red Blockout Tape • Opaquing Markers

LETRAPAQUE MASKING FILM is available in 2 colors, photo red (for straightforward applications) and vivid red (for greater cutting visibility). This ultra-thin film is easy to cut, for clean edges and corners. Its low-tack adhesive facilitates correct registration; it is possible to reposition film several times even after burnishing. Available in sheets of 10″ × 13″ and 20″ × 26″.

LETRAMASK FILM comes in 20″ × 26″ sheets, available in red and amber. This is a readily strippable film, designed specifically for color separation, silhouettes and windows.

LETRALINE RED BLOCKOUT TAPE an excellent quality masking film for quick and simple laying of lines and boxes, offers the same high level of photo opacity as Letrapaque Masking Film. Available in widths of 2 pt., 4 pt., 8 pt., 12 pt., 18 pt. and 24 pt.. all rolls are 650″ in length.

OPAQUING MARKERS give strippers the choice of broad and fine nibs, ideal for working with photo film for maximum effectiveness.

To enter the Grand Prize Drawing, simply complete the Entry Form at right, answering the questions about Letraset products (answers can all be found in this mailing).

BEAT THE JUNE 30, 1985 DEADLINE FOR EXTRA CHANCES TO WIN IN THE BONUS QUARTERLY DRAWING!!

THE SECOND QUARTERLY BONUS DRAWING

Here's what you could win in our second Bonus Drawing—remember, you've got to beat the 6/30/85 deadline to be eligible to win!

FIRST PRIZE

1 AWARDED—Fisher Complete State-of-the-Art Stereo System

SECOND PRIZE

2 Awarded—Fisher Portable Stereo System

THIRD PRIZE

5 Awarded—SONY FM Stereo Walkman

Your completed and mailed entry form doubles as an entry in both the Grand Prize Drawing and—provided it's received by the deadline—also the Bonus Quarterly Drawing!

OFFICIAL RULES

1. No purchase necessary. Simply complete official entry blank per instructions, hand printing your name, address, and zip code in plain block letters. You may obtain an official entry form by submitting an official "Sign Up" form provided by Letraset USA, or by writing to 1985 Letraset "Destination Hawaii" Entry Form, P.O. Box 621, Lowell, IN 46399.
2. Mail your entry to Letraset "Destination Hawaii", P.O. Box 503, Lowell, Ind. 46399. Only one entry per individual per month. Only official entry forms will be accepted. All entries must be received by December 1, 1985. Not responsible for lost, illegible, misdirected or late mail.
3. Winners will be selected from among all entries received in random drawings conducted by VENTURA ASSOCIATES, INC., an independent judging organization whose decisions are final. By entering this sweepstakes entrants agree to, and accept these rules. Winners will be notified by mail and may be required to sign and return an affidavit of eligibility within 21 days of date on notification. If completed affidavit is not received within 21 days, alternate winner may be selected. Winners agree to use of their names and likenesses without additional compensation.
4. Quarterly drawings, in addition to the grand drawing to be held after December 31, 1985, will be held, and quarterly bonus prizes will be awarded. Winners will be drawn from those official entries submitted during each quarter. Deadlines for quarterly entries are March 31, 1985, June 30, 1985, and September 30, 1985. Winners will be notified in the month following the drawing deadline.
5. Grand Prize Hawaiian vacation includes round-trip air-fare to Hawaii, first class hotel accommodations for two for seven days, plus $500 cash. Travel Prize is subject to space and departure availability and must be taken by Dec. 31, 1986. Three (3) first prizes consist of 19″ TV, VCR and video camera. Five (5) second prize winners will receive Vitamaster System 1 (7000) exercise machine. Ten (10) third prize winners will receive a Structo Portable Gas Grill. One thousand (1,000) fourth prizes of a Letraset Digital Desk Clock will be awarded.
6. This sweepstakes is open to residents of the United States, 18 years of age and older who sell Letraset products, employed by authorized Letraset retail distributors. Void where prohibited by law. All federal, state and local laws and regulations apply. Employees and their families of Letraset USA Inc., its parent, subsidiaries, and affiliates, and their advertising, and promotion agencies and VENTURA ASSOCIATES, INC., are not eligible. No duplicate major prize winners. No substitution for prizes except as necessary due to prize availability. Taxes are the responsibility of the winners. Odds of winning determined by number of eligible entries received.
7. For a list of major prize winners, send a stamped, self-addressed envelope to Letraset "Destination Hawaii" Winners, P.O. Box 727, Lowell, IN 46399.

LETRASET "DESTINATION HAWAII" SWEEPSTAKES

E N T R Y   F O R M

☐ **YES!** Enter me in the Letraset "Destination Hawaii" Sweepstakes: I've answered all of the questions below and completed the form.

☐ **YES!** I've beaten the deadline of June 30, 1985. Enter me in the Bonus Quarterly Drawing, and let me know if I'm a winner! I understand that this Drawing will take place early in July.

1. Letrapaque Masking film is available in 2 colors, _____ (for straightforward applications) and _____ (for greater cutting visibility).
2. Letramask Film is a readily strippable film, designed specifically for _____, silhouettes and windows.
3. Letraline Red Blockout Tape is available in _____ point sizes, all in 650″ long rolls.
4. Opaquing Markers are available in broad and _____ nibs

FIRST QUARTER WINNERS

FIRST PRIZE

Mark Corrigan
Multicraft Inc.
Shaker Hts., OH

SECOND PRIZE

David Hoffman
Sam Flax Art Supply
New York, NY

Sharon Kraynak
North Penn Art
Lansdale, PA

THIRD PRIZE

Dennis Hickey
Colorcrafters
Levittown, PA

Mitch Kelemen
Simmons
Art Supplies, Inc.
Scottsdale, AZ

Wendy Miller
Seattle Art
Seattle, WA

Juliana Terada
Swain's Graphics
Glendale, CA

Laura Weiss
Wyoming Paint
Scranton, PA

Name _____

Retail Store _____

Address _____

City _____ State _____ Zip _____

Courtesy of Letraset U.S.A.

3. Name the Sweepstakes

Along with the sponsor's name comes the sweepstakes' name (see Illustration 34). As we have stressed, it is essential to put together a sweepstakes that ties every element to the product you are selling. This starts with the name and theme of the offer. Your goal in choosing the name of the sweepstakes is to be sure all parts of the promotion fit together logically and that your sweepstakes name represents your product well. Following the sponsor's name comes the name of the sweepstakes. For example, you would write: "Acme Products Presents the You're the Tops Sweepstakes" (Acme being a synonym for pinnacle, top, best, etc.). Splash your sweepstakes name prominently on the page and carry the theme of the sweepstakes throughout your creative presentation.

4. State the Number of Prizes

Following the sweepstakes name, you generally blast the huge number of prizes that are being offered (see Illustration 35). As mentioned in Chapter Six, using a pyramidal prize structure in which you offer thousands of low-end prizes allows you to promote a really big number to attract participants. You can say, "OVER 10,000 PRIZES GUARANTEED TO BE AWARDED!" or "OVER 10,000 CHANCES TO WIN!" The larger the number of prizes you offer, the more prominently that number can be displayed. One recent sweepstakes announced: "OVER 88,000 PRIZES IN ALL!" This was stated over and over in all the advertising. It had the power to make people feel that they were definitely going to win a prize because there were so many prizes available. The result was a tremendous number of entries.

5. Describe the Prize

Then comes the real meat of your sweepstakes—what participants can win. Because your sweepstakes has been properly designed, you will have several levels of prizes, from the Grand Prize through the third, fourth, fifth, and maybe even sixth

ILLUSTRATION 34 American Express "Prizes Worth Waiting For" Sweepstakes, Magazine Insert

Never let a prospect wonder who is sponsoring the sweepstakes or what the sweepstakes name is. This magazine insert for American Express, created by Ventura Associates, makes this clear.

Courtesy of American Express.

ILLUSTRATION 35 Great American Magazines, Inc., Certificate of Eligibility

The sponsor plays up the two most important elements in a prize structure: the big first prizes and the total number of prizes. Note the effective use of the key copy lines: "One Million Dollar Grand Prize Winner" and "Over 25,000 Prizes Guaranteed to Be Awarded."

Courtesy of Great American Magazines, Inc.

prize. The Grand Prize should generate the most excitement for your offer. In fact, since it is the prize that costs the most, it's the basket into which you've placed most of your eggs, so you should give it the most space in your prize description. In terms of emphasis, you should devote about 50 percent of the prize area of your material to the big prize. Pictures of the Grand Prize accompanied by exciting, benefit-laden copy should be used to create excitement for your offer. If your Grand Prize consists of more than one item or is a choice of several big items, you may want to give it even more space in your presentation. Generally, the descriptive copy that accompanies the prize presentation should take up far less room than the visual representation, which should be quite extensive. People are more interested in seeing what they can win than reading about it (see Illustration 36).

ILLUSTRATION 36 Doane's Great American Agriculture Sweepstakes, *New Woman* On the Go Sweepstakes, United Virginia Bank Premier VISA Card Sweepstakes.

Ventura Associates followed the Basic Formula for sweepstakes creative exactly, devoting a lot of space to the Grand Prize in these sweepstakes brochures. United Virginia Bank's sweepstakes brochure did much the same thing to produce this very upscale and elegant piece.

Courtesy of Doane's Agricultural Report.

ILLUSTRATION 36 *(concluded)*

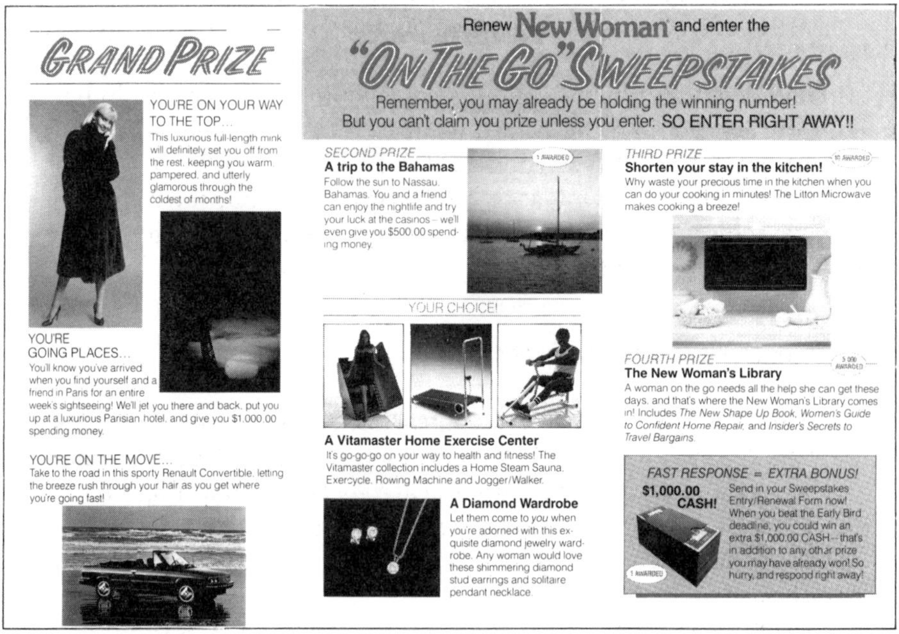

Courtesy of *New Woman* Magazine.

Courtesy of United Virginia Bank.

The description of the Grand Prize is followed by the other prizes; the higher up in the prize structure they are, the greater emphasis they should be given. When you get down to the prizes at the lowest end (which should be very inexpensive and in huge quantities), you may not even want to picture them. Rather, you might say, "10,000 Awarded—Fifth Prize—Three-Volume Cookbook Set," and follow it with body copy. After all, the major reason we include so many low-end prizes is to make the number of chances to win greater.

6. Tell Them How to Enter

Next in your sweepstakes presentation you tell the participants how to "play." While this is sometimes included in the official rules, it is better to devote a separate section explaining how entrants can participate. This gives you an opportunity to include more product sell and point participants in the direction of the product.

If an entrant must go through a series of steps in order to participate in the sweepstakes, you should take them through these one by one with each step numbered in logical sequence. This helps to organize the information, enabling participants to assimilate it more quickly. Making the entry process easier will increase participation in your sweepstakes, helping to build awareness of your product and generate more sales (see Illustration 37).

7. State the Rules of the Game

The final item in the creative presentation of your sweepstakes is the official rules. The rules are a required element in prize promotion material of all types. They carry all of the legal requirements and are necessary, of course; but remember, they don't sell your sweepstakes, and they don't move goods off the shelf. So, generally, the rules are written in small type—as small as possible while remaining readable.

While most official rules begin with, "No purchase necessary," it is preferable to state, "No purchase required." It's a stronger statement, and it subliminally suggests that entrants

ILLUSTRATION 37 Official Rules: Norwegian Caribbean Lines Cruise through Life Sweepstakes, HBO Great Invitation Sweepstakes, Lawson Hill "Road to Riches" Sweepstakes.

While the official rules are required in every sweepstakes presentation, they are not usually emphasized. Plain black mouse type is the order of the day for sweepstakes brochures for Norwegian Caribbean Lines, Home Box Office, and Lawson Hill in pieces created by Ventura Associates.

OFFICIAL RULES

1. Each individual booking for a seven night Norwegian Caribbean Lines cruise for which a deposit is received and processed between July 1, 1985 and September 30, 1985 qualifies for automatic entry in the NCL Cruise Through Life Travel Agent Sweepstakes. Group and interline bookings are not eligible.
2. The number of entries per eligible booking will be determined as follows:

   SINGLE ENTRY—Each booking on the M/S Starward, the M/S Southward, or the M/S Skyward.

   TWO ENTRIES—Each booking on the S/S Norway for stateroom category rates 6–16.

   FOUR ENTRIES—Each booking on the S/S Norway for stateroom category rates 1–5.

   DOUBLE BONUS ENTRIES—Each booking for a seven night cruise with a sailing date in September, 1985 will be worth double the normal number of entries outlined above.
3. Sweepstakes open only to travel agencies within the United States and to their travel counselors. To be eligible to receive a prize, a travel counselor must be employed at the travel agency at which the cruise was booked at the time of prize awarding. Employees and their families of Norwegian Caribbean Lines, their subsidiaries and affiliates, their advertising and production agencies and VENTURA ASSOCIATES, INC., are not eligible. Offer void where prohibited or restricted by law.
4. Winners will be selected in random drawings conducted by VENTURA ASSOCIATES, INC., an independent judging organization whose decisions are final. Prizes will be awarded by random selection during the course of the program. All prizes guaranteed to be awarded.
5. Winners will be notified by mail and may, to receive a prize, be required to sign and return an affidavit of release and eligibility within 14 days of the date on notification or alternate winning entries may be selected. Winners agree to the use of their names and likenesses for publicity and advertising purposes.
6. The Grand Prize winner will receive use each year of equivalent make and model of the car selected from among the cars offered the first year. If same car is not available a car of similar value or cash value of the 1986 lease will be substituted each year at the discretion of the independent judging organization. The Grand Prize of a new car every year for life is predicated on the return of the previous year's car to the lessor in acceptable condition or in comparable condition to cars of the same age based on industry standards. Winner may be required to show a valid driver's license each year on new car award date. Insurance, maintenance, operating expenses and plates are responsibility of winner. Prizes are non-transferable. No substitutions for any prize.
7. For agencies which have rules or policies governing incentive award programs, NCL will abide by those policies in handling prize awards to the employees of that agency.

NCL

Ships' Registry Norway

©1985 Ventura Associates, Inc

Courtesy of Norwegian Caribbean Lines.

ILLUSTRATION 37 *(continued)*

NO PURCHASE REQUIRED
OFFICIAL RULES

1. Complete the official entry blank and check the appropriate box, then mail this Official Entry/Order Card. Or print "HBO Sweepstakes," your name and address on a 3" x 5" card and mail.
2. Winners will be selected in random drawings from among all entries received under the supervision of VENTURA ASSOCIATES, INC., an independent judging organization, whose decisions are final. This offer made by Home Box Office, Inc. Various creative presentations of this Sweepstakes may be used. Chances to win will be determined by the number of entries received. One major prize to a family. No substitutions for prizes offered, with the exception of the Grand Prize where, at the sole discretion of the sweepstakes sponsor, the cash award may be substituted. Trip prize must be taken within one year of notification and is subject to availability. Tax liability is solely that of the winner. The following is the approximate retail value of the prizes: Grand Prize = $10,000, Second Prize = $600, Third Prize = $375, Fourth Prize = $200, Fifth Prize = $50, Sixth Prize = $10.
3. All entries must be received by May 15, 1982. Sweepstakes open to residents of the United States except employees and families of Home Box Office, VENTURA ASSOCIATES, INC., and their various affiliates and agencies. It is not necessary to be a Cable or HBO subscriber to win. All federal, state and local regulations apply. Void where prohibited by law. Winners will be notified by mail.
4. For a list of major prize winners, send a separate self-addressed, stamped envelope to Home Box Office Winners, VENTURA ASSOCIATES, INC., 200 Madison Avenue, New York, NY 10016. DO NOT SEND ENTRIES OR OTHER CORRESPONDENCE TO THIS ADDRESS.

**JUST MAIL THE R.S.V.P. CARD
TO GET A CHANCE OF WINNING**

Courtesy of Home Box Office, Inc.

ILLUSTRATION 37 *(concluded)*

OFFICIAL RULES

No purchase required. Winners will be selected in random drawings under the supervision of VENTURA ASSOCIATES, INC., an independent judging organization whose decisions are final. All entries must be received by December 31, 1985. Early Bird prizes will be awarded from all entries received by the date shown elsewhere in this offer. Winners will be notified by mail. One major prize to a family. Prizes won by minors may be awarded to parent or legal guardian. Travel subject to space and departure availability and must be completed by December 31, 1986. Major winners, or if a minor, their parent or legal guardian, will be asked to sign an affidavit of eligibility which must be returned within 14 days of date of notification. Taxes are the responsibility of winners. No substitution for prizes except as offered herein or as may be necessary due to availability.

Sweepstakes open to residents of the U.S., except employees and their families of Ventura Associates, Inc. the cooperating sponsors, or any organizations connected with this sweepstakes. The 1985 Road To Riches Sweepstakes may be offered in different creative presentations. This sweepstakes is sponsored by various independent businesses and direct marketing firms, all of whom share the total cost. Circulation limited to 50 million. Void where prohibited or restricted by law. All federal, state and local regulations apply.

For the names of the major prize winners, send a separate self-addressed, stamped envelope to: Road To Riches Winners List, P.O. Box 774, Lowell, IN 46356. Do not send orders or other correspondence to this address.

HERE'S HOW TO ENTER:

1. Detach the appropriate Entry Sticker from the front of this catalog wrapper and paste it to the front of your non-transferable, personalized Sweepstakes Entry Certificate.
2. Check your Grand Prize preference on the front of the Sweepstakes Entry Certificate.
3. Complete the questionnaire on the reverse side of your Sweepstakes Entry Certificate—remember, all the answers to these questions can easily be found in your Lawson Hill catalog.
4. Enclose your Sweepstakes Entry Certificate, along with any order you're placing, in the handy pre-addressed return envelope. Remember to include postage!

"ROAD TO RICHES" SWEEPSTAKES

OFFICIAL ENTRY CERTIFICATE

COMPLETE QUESTIONNAIRE AND RETURN WITH ORDER.

1. The shoe "Applause" by Contempo, located on page 3, is described as '__________ Style!'
2. On page 14, the shoe "Punch," described as "Cool and Airy, Yet Dressy," is by the designer__________.
3. Page 22 features a coordinated shoe and handbag set, called__________.

THIS IS YOUR LAWSON HILL CREDIT VOUCHER!

Here's all you do to redeem it:

1. Look through our catalog and make your shoe order selections from the hundreds of fashionable styles and brand-name selections available.
2. Endorse your personalized credit voucher, and deduct $5.00 from your order total.
3. Enclose endorsed credit voucher, along with your order form and method of payment, in the pre-addressed return envelope. Or, if you're ordering by phone, we will automatically deduct $5.00 from your order total when you give us your credit voucher number.

X__________

Endorse credit voucher by signing here—valid through June 30, 1985.

Courtesy of Hill Brothers.

should purchase your product if they have any hope of winning. (Of course, there is no truth to this—it's simply a matter of reinforcing what people already believe—that you can't get something for nothing.)

So ends the Basic Formula of sweepstakes creative presentation. Now, let's examine some of the finer points of sweepstakes creative involving several different media.

GAME CARDS, NECKERS, AND HANGTAGS

While the Basic Formula for sweepstakes creative remains the same for these pieces, the presentation is altered considerably because you are working in miniature. Game cards and neckers (pieces that fit around the necks of bottles and jars) are generally quite small, which means you have no room to spare. No matter what the size of the piece, you have to include the official rules. So, you must cram lots of information onto the front of the card because the rules, even if written in the smallest readable type possible, will take up quite a bit of space (see Illustration 38). Invariably, they will fill up all or most of the back. Generally, there is no room on these pieces to show any prizes. In fact, there is no room to even describe prizes beyond a brief mention, such as: "Grand Prize—1986 Pontiac Firebird."

Game cards usually have scratch-off or ruboff spots that should be featured prominently since they are the essence of your promotion. In addition, you must devote a goodly amount of space to telling consumers how to play. Of prime importance in creating game cards is that you make them look like FUN. In fact, the major appeal of game cards is that participants can usually find out *instantly* if they are a winner. Game cards are the ultimate involvement device. They offer immediate gratification, and this point should be emphasized as much and as often as possible. So add to your list of items that must be mentioned on the game card the words WIN INSTANTLY!

FREE-STANDING INSERTS (FSIs) AND SPACE ADS

FSIs are the four-color Sunday supplements that accompany your newspaper. They are very much like space ads in magazines

ILLUSTRATION 38 Game Cards: Horizon Financial Giveaway, Matching Bucks Game, Pet Partners for Prizes Game.

These game cards were created by Ventura Associates for some of its clients. Note how severely we must pare down the creative presentation to fit it all in such a small space.

$30,000
IN INSTANT CASH PRIZES!
Scratch off the panel with a coin or fingernail to see if you are one of thousands of instant winners of $1 up to $500. Take winning card to any teller.
Use this card to enter our drawings for grand prizes and unclaimed prizes.
$30,000
IN GRAND PRIZES!
You could win one of these savings portfolios: $15,000, $10,000 or $5,000. To enter, print your name, address and phone number on the reverse side of this card and deposit in drawing box.
HORIZON
FINANCIAL FA
A SAVINGS INSTITUTION

Courtesy of Horizon Financial.

SUGAR FREE
BREATH SAVERS
PEPPERMINT

SWEET NOTHINGS
FIVE FLAVOR
SUGARLESS CANDY

RETAILER GAME
Win 1, 2 or even more of the 33,510 cash prizes ranging from $1 to $1,000.

Just match a right-half with a left-half of the same value.

Courtesy of Life Savers, Inc.

ILLUSTRATION 38 ***(concluded)***

Courtesy of Superior Pet Products, Inc.

(see Illustration 39), except that they can get greater attention from a consumer because they so often fall out of the newspaper and into his lap! In terms of creative presentation, FSIs and magazine ads are almost identical, and they follow the Basic Formula—with one exception: usually, an entry blank coupon will be included in the lower right corner of the page. (If you're using a left-hand page, it would be the lower left corner of the page.)

When a coupon is used as an entry blank in an FSI or space ad, it must provide space for the entrant's name and address. You should allow plenty of room, with dark lines on white background, to allow people to write legibly. In addition, if you're using programmed learning as part of the entry requirement for your sweepstakes, you'll need to make the entry blank/coupon big enough to accommodate your questions and the entrants' answers. You may also want to have boxes that entrants can check to tell whether or not they've purchased your product.

While FSIs and space ads follow the Basic Formula for sweepstakes presentation, most of them give even greater attention to the Grand Prize than ads in other media. The visuals of the lesser prizes are often eliminated in favor of a big picture of the Grand Prize. After all, you're not dealing with a huge space—generally no more than 7 × 10 or 8½ × 11—and if your Grand Prize is indeed your biggest draw, by all means play it for all it's worth.

ILLUSTRATION 39 American Express Corporate Card Successful Strategies Sweepstakes Space Ad

This space ad ran in magazines directed to the business market. It promoted a business-oriented sweepstakes for American Express created by Ventura Associates.

MANAGEMENT TIPS FOR YOUR SMALL BUSINESS*

The American Express® Corporate Card can be an important tool in managing your business. And to introduce you to the Corporate Card, we're giving you over 100 chances to win some excellent prizes, all geared to furthering the success of your company. It's easy to enter—just fill out the coupon below, and we'll send you information and an American Express Corporate Card application, and enter you automatically in

THE AMERICAN EXPRESS® CORPORATE CARD SUCCESSFUL STRATEGIES SWEEPSTAKES

Here are the exciting prizes you'll get when you're a winner:

GRAND PRIZE —1 AWARDED
BUSINESS CONSULTATION

You'll receive 2 days of consultation with your choice of America's top business consultants. Choose from experts (listed to the right) that can best suit your business needs and specialties:

—KENNETH BLANCHARD: Ph.D., who specializes in productivity management, is chairman of Blanchard Training and Development, and co-author of *The One Minute Manager.*

—JULIAN BLOCK: A tax planning specialist who is the editor of *Recommendations*, a weekly newsletter on tax planning for the Research Institute of America, and author of *Julian Block's Guide to Year Round Tax Savings.*

—JOSEPH R. MANCUSO: founder and director of the Center for Entrepreneurial Management, Inc., and author of fifteen books, including his best seller, *How to Start, Finance and Manage Your Own Small Business.*

—JERRY STRAUSS: founder of the consulting firm, Jerry Strauss and Associates, specializing in management consulting for exceptional productivity, excellence and leadership.

—POWERBASE: a database management company which specializes in determining software needs for the present and for future growth.

SECOND PRIZE —1 AWARDED
THE PANASONIC EASAPHONE™

This total tele-system is an answering machine, telephone, auto dialer and monitor speaker all in one highly styled unit that functions as a dictating machine and 2-way tape recorder as well. All these features to better serve your communication needs and keep your company on the move and growing.

THIRD PRIZE —100 AWARDED
The American Express® Card Calculator

The American Express Card Calculator fits right into your wallet, so it's convenient for traveling and is ready to work when you are. This super-slim 4-function solar calculator operates in any light and never needs batteries.

Benefits abound from the American Express Corporate Card. Among them:

- Total separation of your business and personal charges.
- Accurate and comprehensive documentation for your tax records.
- Quarterly Management Reports
- Reduced cash advances, improved cash flow.
- Reduced administrative time and costs.
- Consolidated billing—one monthly statement, one bill to pay.
- No pre-set spending limit.*
- One card that can cover almost all of your travel and entertainment needs.

*Transactions are approved based on past spending, payment patterns and personal resources.

☐ Yes, enter me in the American Express Corporate Card SUCCESSFUL STRATEGIES Sweepstakes, and send me information and an application for the American Express Corporate Card. I understand I need not purchase anything to enter this Sweepstakes.

☐ No, I would not like to receive information and an application at this time, but please enter me in the American Express Corporate Card SUCCESSFUL STRATEGIES Sweepstakes.

NAME____________________

TITLE____________________

COMPANY____________________

ADDRESS____________________

CITY__________ STATE______ ZIP______

PHONE__________ NO. OF TRAVELERS______

If you don't want to enter the sweepstakes but would like more information about how the American Express Corporate Card can help your small business, call **1-800-528-AMEX** *In Arizona call **602-222-3283**

RETURN COUPON TO:
SUCCESSFUL STRATEGIES SWEEPSTAKES
P.O. BOX 475
Lowell, IN 46356
244-00-0082-6

AMERICAN EXPRESS Travel Management Services®

OFFICIAL RULES
No purchase required, here's all you do:
Complete the Official Entry Form at left and return it to the address indicated. All entries must be received by 2/28/85. Winners will be determined in random drawings on March 1, 1985 from all entries received under the supervision of VENTURA ASSOCIATES, INC., an independent judging organization whose decisions are final. All prizes will be awarded, and winners may be required to sign a letter of eligibility and release within 21 days of notification. Winners' names and likenesses may be used for publicity purposes and each contestant consents to that by participating in the sweepstakes. Winners will be notified by mail. The odds of winning will be determined by the number of entries received. Sweepstakes open to residents of the United States, except where prohibited or restricted by law. All Federal, State, and local regulations apply. Taxes on prizes are sole responsibility of winners. No duplicate winners and substitution of prizes other than may be necessary due to availability will be permitted. Employees and their families of American Express Travel Related Services, Inc., its affiliated companies, its advertising and production agencies, Women's Marketing and Sports, Inc., and VENTURA ASSOCIATES, INC. are not eligible.

For a list of major prize winners, send a stamped, self-addressed envelope to: SUCCESSFUL STRATEGIES Winners' List, P.O. Box 789, Lowell, IN 46356. The list of winners will also be published on the Reader Service Cards in the May issues of WORKING WOMAN and SUCCESS magazines.

Courtesy of American Express.

TELEVISION COMMERCIALS

Sometimes, if a sweepstakes is big enough and exciting enough, the sponsor will run television commercials as support advertising for their offer. Generally, these commercials don't go into great detail since broadcast time is very expensive and the commercials are just one part of the advertising campaign for the sweepstakes.

The "feel" of these commercials should be much like a carnival, the barker blaring out to passersby the fabulous opportunity that will soon be arriving in the mail. These are usually 30-second commercials. However, it is possible to get your message across in 10-second spots, since all you need say is: "WIN $10,000,000.00! American Family Publishers is mailing details! Arriving at your home soon! Your chance to win $10,000,000.00!" There's not much more to it. These commercials are simple and brief—almost teasers—and they generate excitement with the anticipation of the promotion's arrival at the consumers' homes.

There are times, however, when the commercial must tell the whole story of the sweepstakes, necessitating a longer spot. Ventura Associates used television to promote a new book, *Chance of a Lifetime,* written by Bill Adler and published by Warner Books. It is a book about starting a new business, and, in addition, the book itself is a contest! The contest offered $25,000 to the person who came up with the best new business idea, as determined by a panel of judges (Illustration 40). (See Chapter Two for a detailed discussion of judging contests.)

To dramatize the contest—and to support Adler's position as a highly successful entrepreneur—the commercial opened with Adler counting stacks of bills—$25,000 worth. Consistent with the Basic Formula of sweepstakes creative, a voice-over announcer shouted "Bill Adler wants to pay you $25,000!" The commercial then explained the book and told viewers how to participate in the contest. In support of book sales, which was the real objective of this promotion, viewers were directed to the nearest bookstore to purchase the book that could give them their chance of a lifetime!

ILLUSTRATION 40 *Chance of a Lifetime,* Book Cover

Chance of a Lifetime, a book about starting a new business, was a contest in itself. The reader who came up with the best new business idea, selected by a panel of judges, won $25,000—a chance of a lifetime!

DIRECT MAIL

Sweepstakes direct mail packages come in varying intensities. You can have a subtle, quiet sweepstakes overlay to a direct mail package (this is not the most effective use of sweepstakes). You can opt for a sweepstakes package in which all, or nearly all, of the components say "Sweepstakes," though they don't scream it. And you can use the "screamer" package which whips up a frenzy of excitement, setting off bells and whistles, shouting WIN! WIN! WIN! These bells-and-whistles packages are commonly given that demeaning name "junk mail," yet they generate the greatest response when used in the right markets (which leads us to believe that a lot of Americans really adore the mail they demean).

The components of direct mail packages that apply to sweepstakes are as follows.

Outer Envelope

The outer envelope is the carrier of your direct mail package and is therefore the most important part of your mailing. The carrier must not be a barrier. If your prospects aren't sufficiently stimulated to open the envelope, the advertisement inside will be for naught. You will waste your money and lose a perfectly good prospect. Therefore, you must use compelling teasers, windows, and involvement devices to lure your prospects deeper into your offer (see Illustration 41).

A package created by Ventura Associates for the publication *Practical Sailor* presents perhaps the ultimate in compelling teasers. It displayed the classic sweepstakes yes/no stickers through a window in the envelope, and it stated: "While both of these stickers can enter you in the Grand Adventure Sweepstakes, only one of them could save your life." (The basis for this bold assertion was that much of the information covered in *Practical Sailor* is indeed potentially lifesaving for sailors.)

Usually the teaser on the outer envelope acts like a headline in the sweepstakes Basic Formula: it concentrates on the Grand Prize. The other side of the *Practical Sailor* envelope was devoted to the Grand Prize sell, offering recipients a chance to win a trip

ILLUSTRATION 41 *Practical Sailor* Grand Adventure II Sweepstakes Outer Envelope, Window with Yes/No Stickers

On the outer envelope of sweepstakes packages, it is important to come in with your best foot forward, announcing the Grand Prize right up front. This package, done by Ventura Associates for *Practical Sailor,* does just that!

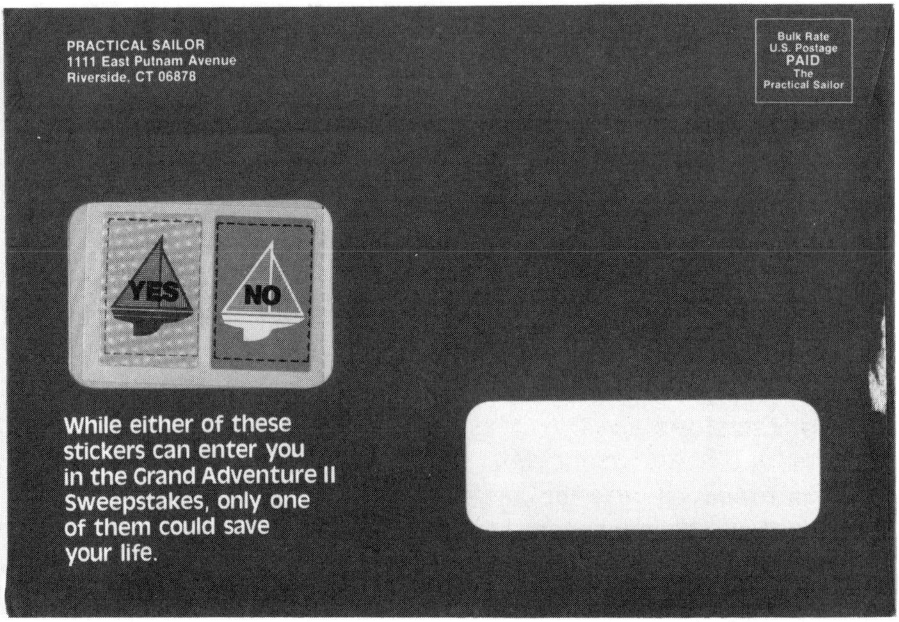

Courtesy of *Practical Sailor,* Belvoir Publications, Inc.

to Perth, Australia, to witness the 1987 America's Cup races (see Illustration 42).

The classic bells-and-whistles envelope should be loaded with many different elements. While it may appear that the sole object is to confuse recipients, these copy-laden envelopes really work. The reason they work is that readers get so *involved* with the envelopes, reading all the little bursts, examining the stamps and the material showing through the windows, and the other official-looking information, that they just have to get inside the package.

ILLUSTRATION 42 *Practical Sailor* Grand Adventure II Sweepstakes Outer Envelope, Window with Grand Prize Teaser

Would you say no to this offer for *Practical Sailor* created by Ventura Associates? The way it's positioned, people will think twice before they select the "no" sticker!

Be our guest in Perth, Australia,
home of the next
America's Cup races, when you're
the Grand Prize Winner...

Courtesy of *Practical Sailor,* Belvoir Publications, Inc.

ILLUSTRATION 43 *Newsweek*'s $103,000 Sweepstakes Outer Envelope

Who can let $50,000.00 slip through their fingers? This direct mail package, created by Ventura Associates for Newsweek, challenges that strongly.

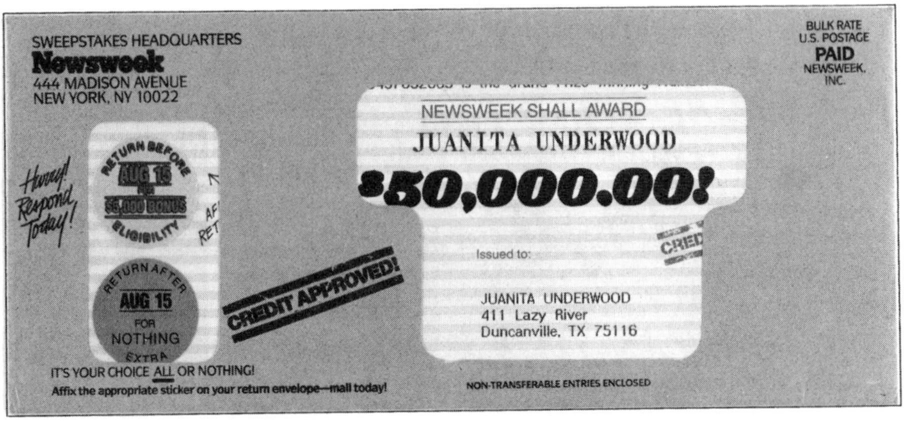

Courtesy of *Newsweek*.

ILLUSTRATION 44 City of Hope National Medical Center Sweepstakes Outer Envelope; *New Woman* On the Go Sweepstakes Outer Envelope.

These outer envelopes let people know loud and clear what they could receive as the Grand Prize winner. The compelling envelopes were created by Ventura Associates for City of Hope National Medical Center and *New Woman.*

Courtesy of City of Hope.

ILLUSTRATION 44 ***(concluded)***

Courtesy of *New Woman* Magazine.

Direct marketers know that personalized packages, such as *Newsweek's* mailing to its college market, help pull recipients in and involve them in the offer. Honestly, if you were Juanita Underwood and you saw: "If 049766311 is the Grand Prize Winning Number, *Newsweek* shall award Juanita Underwood $50,000.00" (see Illustration 43), could you walk away from it? An official-looking document, visible through windows in the outer envelope (and even those hidden inside), make it difficult for the recipient to throw the package away unread (see Illustration 44). Certificates of eligibility, personalized "credit cards," and "checks" payable to the recipient are just a few choices of teaser material (see Illustrations 45, 46a, and 46b).

In addition to strong teasers, the outer envelope generally features the number of prizes being offered (especially if it's a huge number) and a variety of simulated stamps that motivate the recipient to open the envelope. Sometimes there will also be official-looking messages to the postmaster, such as "POSTMASTER: Urgent. Official time-dated sweepstakes entries enclosed—please expedite!" Bringing a federal employee into your offer lends it greater credibility and conveys a sense of urgency and importance.

ILLUSTRATION 45 United Virginia Bank Premier VISA Card Sweepstakes Outer Envelope

The entire thrust of the United Virginia Bank Premier VISA Card Sweepstakes was upscale. The outer envelope has an exceptionally elegant feel. The graphics are attractive, and the teaser copy makes the recipient feel important. These two elements are colorfully presented on the back of the envelope, while the front of the envelope is simple and elegant. This is not a package many people would throw away without reading the contents.

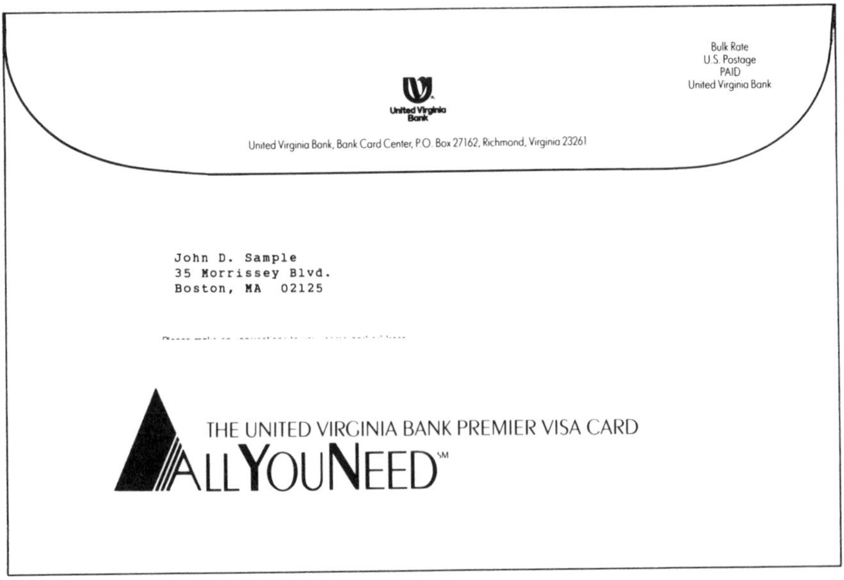

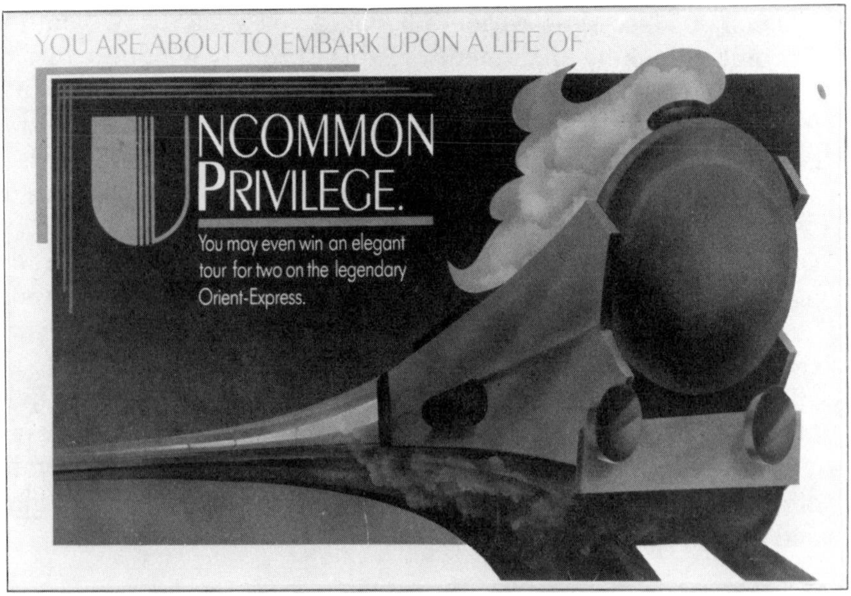

Courtesy of United Virginia Bank.

ILLUSTRATION 46a American Family Publishers Guarantee Document

An official-looking document is hard to throw away. Fully half of all third-class mail in the United States is thrown out unopened. Sweepstakes help to get readership of direct mail.

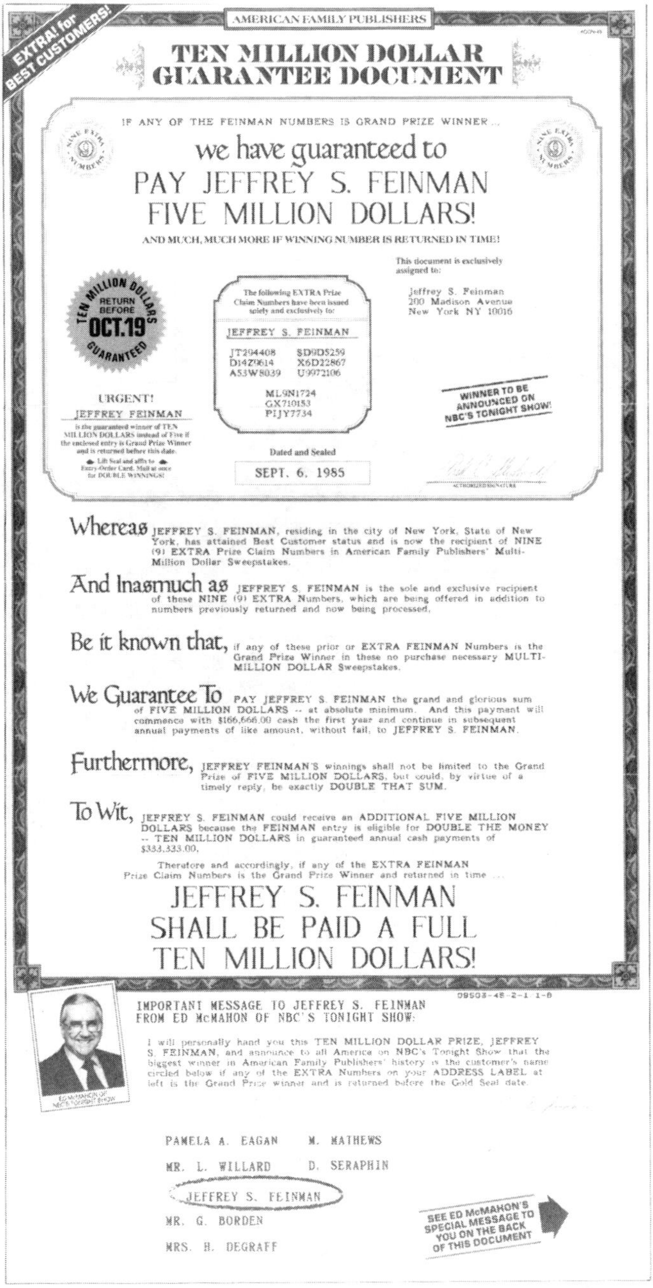

EXTRA! for BEST CUSTOMERS!

AMERICAN FAMILY PUBLISHERS

TEN MILLION DOLLAR GUARANTEE DOCUMENT

IF ANY OF THE FEINMAN NUMBERS IS GRAND PRIZE WINNER...

we have guaranteed to

PAY JEFFREY S. FEINMAN

FIVE MILLION DOLLARS!

AND MUCH, MUCH MORE IF WINNING NUMBER IS RETURNED IN TIME!

TEN MILLION DOLLARS RETURN BEFORE OCT. 19 GUARANTEED

The following EXTRA Prize Claim Numbers have been issued solely and exclusively to:

JEFFREY S. FEINMAN

JT294408 SD9D5259
D14Z9614 X6D22867
A53W8039 U9972106

ML9N1724
GX710153
PIJY7734

This document is exclusively assigned to:

Jeffrey S. Feinman
200 Madison Avenue
New York NY 10016

URGENT!

JEFFREY FEINMAN

is the guaranteed winner of TEN MILLION DOLLARS instead of Five if the enclosed entry is Grand Prize Winner and is returned before this date.

Lift Seal and affix to Entry-Order Card. Mail at once for DOUBLE WINNINGS!

Dated and Sealed

SEPT. 6, 1985

WINNER TO BE ANNOUNCED ON NBC'S TONIGHT SHOW!

AUTHORIZED SIGNATURE

Whereas JEFFREY S. FEINMAN, residing in the city of New York, State of New York, has attained Best Customer status and is now the recipient of NINE (9) EXTRA Prize Claim Numbers in American Family Publishers' Multi-Million Dollar Sweepstakes.

And Inasmuch as JEFFREY S. FEINMAN is the sole and exclusive recipient of these NINE (9) EXTRA Numbers, which are being offered in addition to numbers previously returned and now being processed,

Be it known that, if any of these prior or EXTRA FEINMAN Numbers is the Grand Prize Winner in these no purchase necessary MULTI-MILLION DOLLAR Sweepstakes.

We Guarantee To PAY JEFFREY S. FEINMAN the grand and glorious sum of FIVE MILLION DOLLARS -- at absolute minimum. And this payment will commence with $166,666.00 cash the first year and continue in subsequent annual payments of like amount, without fail, to JEFFREY S. FEINMAN.

Furthermore, JEFFREY FEINMAN'S winnings shall not be limited to the Grand Prize of FIVE MILLION DOLLARS, but could, by virtue of a timely reply, be exactly DOUBLE THAT SUM.

To Wit, JEFFREY S. FEINMAN could receive an ADDITIONAL FIVE MILLION DOLLARS because the FEINMAN entry is eligible for DOUBLE THE MONEY -- TEN MILLION DOLLARS in guaranteed annual cash payments of $333,333.00.

Therefore and accordingly, if any of the EXTRA FEINMAN Prize Claim Numbers is the Grand Prize Winner and returned in time ...

JEFFREY S. FEINMAN
SHALL BE PAID A FULL
TEN MILLION DOLLARS!

09503-45-2-1-1-8

IMPORTANT MESSAGE TO JEFFREY S. FEINMAN
FROM ED McMAHON OF NBC'S TONIGHT SHOW:

ED McMAHON OF NBC'S TONIGHT SHOW

I will personally hand you this TEN MILLION DOLLAR PRIZE, JEFFREY S. FEINMAN, and announce to all America on NBC's Tonight Show that the biggest winner in American Family Publishers' history is the customer's name circled below if any of the EXTRA Numbers on your ADDRESS LABEL at left is the Grand Prize winner and is returned before the Gold Seal date.

PAMELA A. EAGAN M. MATHEWS

MR. L. WILLARD D. SERAPHIN

JEFFREY S. FEINMAN

MR. G. BORDEN

MRS. H. DEGRAFF

SEE ED McMAHON'S SPECIAL MESSAGE TO YOU ON THE BACK OF THIS DOCUMENT

Courtesy of American Family Publishers.

ILLUSTRATION 46b Outer Envelope with Check Showing through Window

A check visible in the window of this envelope makes it difficult to throw away. An effective way to say "big award" is by mailing the check first class.

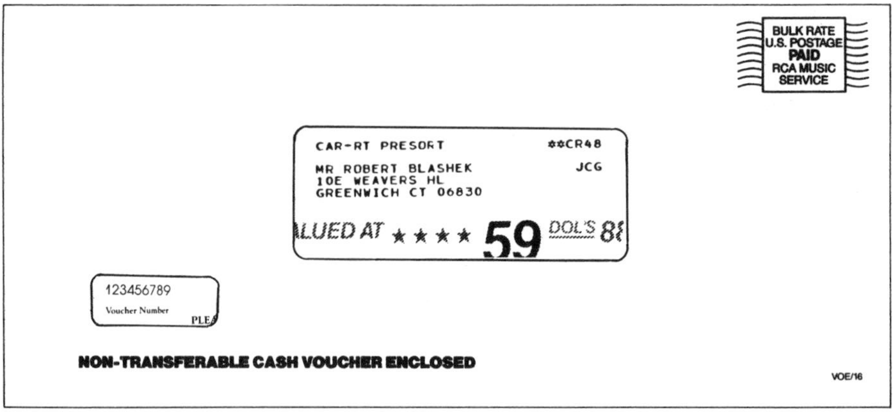

Letter

Whether you're dealing with a one-, two-, or four-page letter, you will still follow the same Basic Formula for creative. Play up the sweepstakes, concentrating on your Grand Prize, but also mention your other fabulous prizes and all the chances your recipient has to win. Next, go into the product sell, pointing up the benefits of your product. Then return to the sweepstakes, reminding prospects to enter by the specified date. End of letter. Well, not quite. Perhaps you'll have a P.S. that reinforces some part of your message or expands on it to make the whole presentation even more compelling.

Naturally, the tone of your letter will reflect the tone of your sweepstakes. For an upscale sweepstakes, the tone of the letter should be very dignified. In a mass market mailing for a mid- to downscale product, you could really go all out in your letter and stir up lots of excitement. In addition, an official-looking personalized certificate or bond right in the letter lends credibility to the offer (see Illustration 47).

ILLUSTRATION 47 Great American Magazines, Inc., Great American Sweepstakes, Certificate of Eligibility with $1,500,000 Bond

To deal with consumer "doubt," note the effective use of the bond on this computer letter.

Courtesy of Great American Magazines, Inc.

Sweepstakes Brochure

This is the piece that displays all your prizes. Keeping in mind the Basic Formula, you should use big color pictures of your Grand Prize and all the others. For many years, the tradition seemed to honor the rule that: "the bigger the sweepstakes, the larger the prize brochure." Today this is not always the case. Great American Magazines, which runs a major sweepstakes in terms of size and the number of prizes they offer, successfully utilized a fairly small sweepstakes brochure. (See Illustration 30 in Chapter Six.) Others, however, are continuing to use a huge four-color brochures to accomplish a more complete sell of their prizes. Both methods can be effective, depending on your presentation and your market. Testing is recommended to determine which one will work best for you.

While the main focus of the sweepstakes brochure is on prizes, the back cover usually carries the official rules as well. Sometimes, the brochure will also carry product and sweepstakes sell (see Illustration 48).

Response Device

The response device is both your entry form and your order form. Generally, in direct mail your aim is to close the sale right then and there. Because of this, you want to compel your recipients not only to enter the sweepstakes but to say yes to your product as well. Because you cannot require purchase with a sweepstakes entry, many people enter the sweepstakes without a thought of buying. This is where the yes/no psychology comes in to play.

Somewhere in your direct mail package you will want an involvement device that encourages prospects to buy your product and discourages them from just entering without buying. This device can be a perforated token or a peel-off sticker that can be affixed to the outer envelope or the response device. This is where yes/no stickers come in. Psychological research tells us that people really like to be good and please others. In essence,

ILLUSTRATION 48 *Sports Illustrated* Super-Sport-Stakes, Sweepstakes Brochure

Sports Illustrated's sweepstakes brochure presented some exciting prizes to sports fans in a graphic style designed to appeal especially to them. Created by Ventura Associates for *Sports Illustrated* Magazine.

they like saying yes and they don't feel good when they have to say no (see Illustration 49). (In fact, in the 1970s there was a successful pop psychology book called, *When I Say No I Feel Guilty.*)

In the direct mail packages created by Ventura Associates for *Newsweek,* participants saying yes to a subscription didn't even have to use a pencil or pen to order or enter the sweepstakes. Most of the pertinent information was already computer-personalized on the form. To place an order, all recipients had to do was punch out little perforated circles from the form and mail it back—easy, very easy.

ILLUSTRATION 48 *(continued)*

An entrant may have to check boxes on an order form to declare his intentions: "☐ Yes, enter me in the Super Duper Sweepstakes. My order is enclosed. Tell me if I'm a winner!" or "☐ No. I'm not ordering, enter me anyway." The YES option is usually in a bright, happy color, while the NO option is in a drab, utterly depressing color.

Another item often used on the response device is a speed motivator—the Early Bird Drawing deadline. If a respondent wants to be eligible for this bonus drawing, he or she must send in the entry by a specified date. The entry form will have a box for them to check near the statement: "I beat the Early Bird date of 11/15/86—enter me in your Early Bird Drawing, too, for extra chances to win!"

ILLUSTRATION 48 ***(concluded)***

Sports Illustrated Super-Sports-Stakes. Courtesy of TIME Inc. Reprinted by permission.

Return Envelope

The first rule of thumb for return envelopes is that they should require postage in order to be delivered. Paying the postage for a recipient who may not buy your product and is just taking advantage of an opportunity to win your fabulous prizes can be very expensive, with no benefit to you. And yet you must present the same chance to enter to buyers and nonbuyers alike, so you can't pay postage for one group and not for the others.

Beyond this, you should take what we know about yes/no psychology and use it on your return envelope as well. It may seem ridiculous, but many people don't want even their postman to know that they're taking advantage of an offer and trying to get something for nothing! While you don't want to humiliate consumers, you can play upon this human weakness to achieve the results you desire—a purchase. This can be accomplished in several ways. Some sweepstakes sponsors, such as *Newsweek,*

ILLUSTRATION 49 *New Woman* On the Go Sweepstakes Response Card; Doane's Agricultural Service Entry/Order Card.

Response devices should be easy to say yes to and difficult to say no to. These pieces, created by Ventura Associates for Doane's Agricultural Report and *New Woman* Magazine, do just that.

WIN

New Woman "On the Go"

SWEEPSTAKES ENTRY/RENEWAL FORM

☐ YES! Enter me in the Sweepstakes! Renew my subscription for 1 year—that's 12 issues for only $12.00

☐ YES! YES! I want 2 more years of New Woman at your *lowest rate*—24 issues for $22.00 (only 92¢ per issue!).

YOUR PRESELECTED SWEEPSTAKES ENTRY NO.

HK 301 562

0 560004 K0G 0005W095 66W1 24 P 3K
SEP85
GRACE KROGH *****
5D WOODBINE AV **3DG
AVENEL NJ 07001

EARLY BIRD
$1,000.00 BONUS

☐ YES! I'm responding by:

06/01/85

Enter me in the Early Bird Drawing, too!

☐ Payment enclosed. (Make checks payable to New Woman.)

☐ Bill me.

☐ No. I'm not renewing, but enter me anyway.

Rates apply to U.S., U.S. Possessions, APO-FPO addresses only. All foreign subscriptions must be prepaid. Add $4.00 each year for Canada. $10.00 for each year for foreign.

3K-C1-RSW

Courtesy of *New Woman* Magazine.

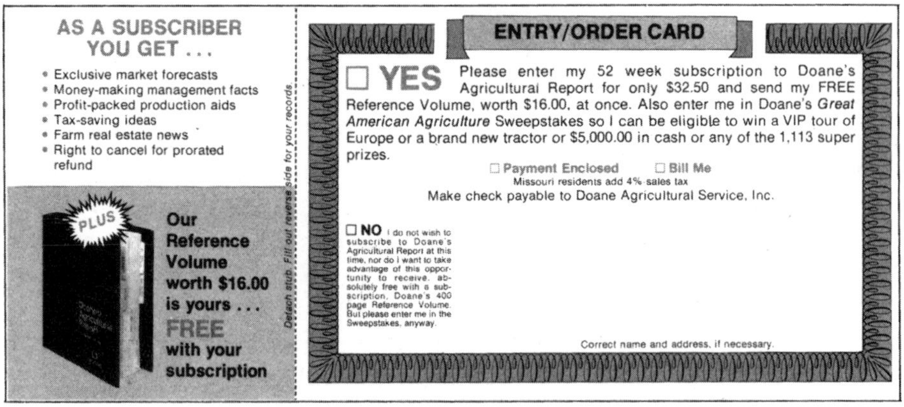

AS A SUBSCRIBER YOU GET . . .

- Exclusive market forecasts
- Money-making management facts
- Profit-packed production aids
- Tax-saving ideas
- Farm real estate news
- Right to cancel for prorated refund

PLUS

Our Reference Volume worth $16.00 is yours . . . FREE with your subscription

Detach stub. Fill out reverse side for your records.

ENTRY/ORDER CARD

☐ YES Please enter my 52 week subscription to Doane's Agricultural Report for only $32.50 and send my FREE Reference Volume, worth $16.00, at once. Also enter me in Doane's *Great American Agriculture* Sweepstakes so I can be eligible to win a VIP tour of Europe or a brand new tractor or $5,000.00 in cash or any of the 1,113 super prizes.

☐ Payment Enclosed ☐ Bill Me

Missouri residents add 4% sales tax

Make check payable to Doane Agricultural Service, Inc.

☐ NO I do not wish to subscribe to Doane's Agricultural Report at this time, nor do I want to take advantage of this opportunity to receive, absolutely free with a subscription, Doane's 400 page Reference Volume. But please enter me in the Sweepstakes, anyway.

Correct name and address, if necessary.

Courtesy of Doane's Agricultural Report.

ILLUSTRATION 50 Return Envelopes: *New Woman* "On the Go" Sweepstakes, *Newsweek's* $103,000 Sweepstakes, *Practical Sailor* Grand Adventure II Sweepstakes, and *Sports Illustrated* Super-Sports-Stakes.

Whether to say yes or no is always the question in direct mail. These envelopes, the last contact respondents will have with a specific direct mail package, encourage yes responses.

YES! Enter me in the Sweepstakes! My renewal is enclosed!
NO. I'm not renewing, but enter me anyway.
Sweepstakes Headquarters
New Woman
P.O. Box 5243
Boulder, CO 80322
RUSH!
Dated Sweepstakes Entry Enclosed

Courtesy of *New Woman* Magazine.

have separate yes and no envelopes by which the respondent's intentions are immediately obvious for all the world to see. Other sponsors, such as *New Woman* Magazine, keep their return envelope costs down by using just one envelope and asking respondents to state their intentions by checking either a yes box or a no box. Again, the yes is in a happier, brighter color than the no (see Illustration 50).

This has been just a peek under the flap of the circus tent—a glimpse of the legerdemain employed by prize promotion specialists. Ad agencies create ads. Clever ad agencies create clever ads. But it takes a prize promotion specialist to create the kinds of ads and collateral material that explain and entice and turn a passive reader into an active participant.

ILLUSTRATION 50 *(continued)*

Newsweek's
$103,000.00
SWEEPSTAKES

YES!!

Enter me in NEWSWEEK'S
$103,000.00
SWEEPSTAKES
and let me know if I've won—
my subscription to Newsweek
is enclosed!

ON YOUR E-Z WINNER VERIFICATION FORM DID YOU:

- ☑ Check the "YES" box
- ☑ Punch your preferred terms
- ☑ Punch your payment method
- ☑ Punch your graduation year
- ☑ Confirm your address

DETACH HERE. MAIL ONLY ONE ENVELOPE

Newsweek's
$103,000.00
SWEEPSTAKES

NO

I'm not subscribing.
Enter me anyway.

Courtesy of *Newsweek.*

ILLUSTRATION 50 *(continued)*

☐ **YES!** Enter me in the Grand Adventure II Sweepstakes — my subscription to PRACTICAL SAILOR is enclosed. Let me know if I'm going to Australia to watch the races!

☐ **NO.** I'm not ordering. Enter me anyway.

Post Office Will Not Deliver Without Sufficient Postage

Sweepstakes Finals
PRACTICAL SAILOR®
1111 East Putnam Avenue
Riverside, CT 06878

Courtesy of *Practical Sailor,* Belvoir Publications, Inc.

ILLUSTRATION 50 *(concluded)*

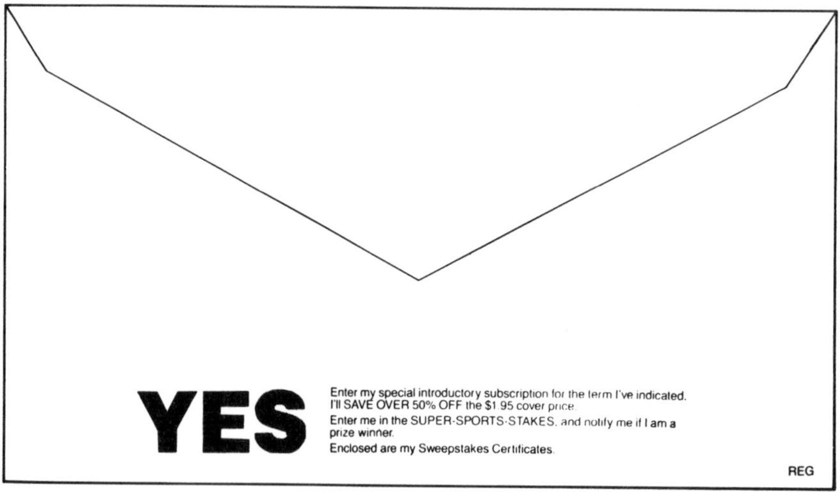
YES
Enter my special introductory subscription for the term I've indicated.
I'll SAVE OVER 50% OFF the $1.95 cover price.
Enter me in the SUPER-SPORTS-STAKES, and notify me if I am a prize winner.
Enclosed are my Sweepstakes Certificates.
REG

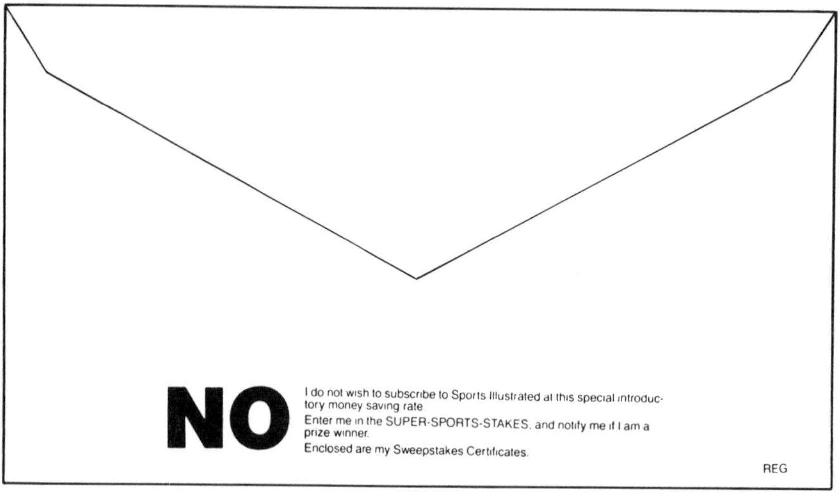
NO
I do not wish to subscribe to Sports Illustrated at this special introductory money saving rate.
Enter me in the SUPER-SPORTS-STAKES, and notify me if I am a prize winner.
Enclosed are my Sweepstakes Certificates.
REG

Sports Illustrated Super-Sports-Stakes. Courtesy of TIME Inc. Reprinted by permission.

CHAPTER EIGHT

The Future of Prize Promotions

There have been detractors of the prize promotion industry since time immemorial. Even when the first lottery was run centuries ago, there undoubtedly were predictions of its early demise. Nevertheless, today all indications point to the continuing growth of prize promotions as a marketing tool.

Several factors will contribute to the growth of prize promotions of all kinds. First, is a new liberal atmosphere. Until recently, the regulatory climate was such that unless the rules made it clear that the nonbuyer could play the game with the same ease as the buyer, the offer was considered illegal. Until the early 1980s, the key legal term was *equal dignity.* That is, buyers and nonbuyers had to be able to enter a prize competition with the same ease and dignity. Obviously, this worked against the marketer. "Equal dignity" reached such significant proportions that a marketer could not run an on-package sweepstakes because the regulatory agencies held that it would be embarrassing for consumers to have to pick up a package and copy down the address and the rules to enter. Therefore, they would, in effect, have been "forced" to buy the product if they wished to participate. Today, things have changed so that we can even pack game tickets inside the packages.

Second, prize offers will continue to grow because of the increasing involvement of state governments in lotteries. The fact that some 23 states operate lotteries today—and it is anticipated that 40 states will have them over the next four years—has cloaked the prize promotion business in respectability. Furthermore, as each year goes by, consumers come to know firsthand people who have actually won major prizes. Familiarity with prize winners is closely related to the modeling principal of psychology—the ability to identify with someone like you.

There is yet another reason for the continuing popularity of sweepstakes. Since the congressional investigation of sweepstakes in the 1970s, consumers have gained increasing confidence that promotion prizes are, in fact, awarded. Self-policing by the prize promotion industry and strict adherence to state regulations guaranteeing the awarding of prizes have helped to ensure that the abuses of the past will not persist. A study conducted in 1985 indicated that 90 percent of the consumers surveyed believed that promotion prizes were awarded fairly. This shows a dramatic increase over a study some 10 years earlier in which less than half the population believed that these offers were conducted honestly. The survival of the prize promotion industry depends on constant reaffirmation that the industry is carefully regulated, providing the positive image necessary to encourage maximum participation by consumers.

The sophistication of consumer market testing has enhanced the development of prize promotion. The practitioner can now definitively predict the success of his offer, whereas, as recently as five years ago, marketers could only guess whether or not consumers were positively disposed to their prize offers. The results of various market tests allow us to say without hesitation that prize promotions are one of the most efficient uses of marketing dollars. A recent *Business Week* article compared McDonald's success with that of Burger King. The article pointed out that McDonald's spends more on promotion than it does on advertising, while at Burger King the situation is reversed. McDonald's is one of the most prolific and aggressive users of prize promotions.

Finally, the future looks even brighter in view of the clutter that exists in other marketing techniques. Because of the significant increase in advertising, it is becoming increasingly difficult to attract and hold the consumer's attention. In view of this, the chance to win a valuable prize will continue to stand out.

Of course, critics of prize promotion might say that in a marketplace where everyone is running contests, they will lose their effectiveness. Our experience tells us that this is not true. As more sweepstakes are run, and consumers become more familiar with the technique, their popularity appears to grow. This is referred to in the industry as the "Las Vegas Effect"—the more hotels that open in Las Vegas, the more the market expands, where conventional wisdom might predict that each would get a smaller share of the pie.

In the future, we can also look forward to even more sophisticated methods of postpromotion research. This is probably the industry's most important area of opportunity. At present overwhelming evidence indicates that consumers give unreliable data when asked to participate in prize promotion research. For example, we constantly hear from focus groups consisting exclusively of people whose names have come from sweepstakes entry blanks that the individuals within the group would *not* enter a sweepstakes! This problem exists in all areas of market research. When questioned about the television programs they regularly watch, viewers invariably try to better their image. They tell researchers that they watch "Meet the Press" when they really watch "Gilligan's Island" reruns! Viewers want to appear sophisticated; consumers who participate in sweepstakes don't want to appear greedy.

However, we are now developing special research techniques that elicit accurate information from consumers. For example, data scanning and other computer techniques can specifically overlay ZIP Codes and reveal numbers of entries by particular income brackets. Eye focus studies measure what parts of ads consumers are actually reading. The use of these new techniques by the prize promotion industry will mean not only increasing recognition of prize promotions as a viable marketing tool but will give marketers a better understanding of the types of promotions that work and those that don't. In addition, we will all have a better idea of what needs to be done to maximize the effectiveness of a particular offer.

Another dramatic change that will help ensure a bright future for prize promotion is the birth of co-op sweepstakes. In this type of program, a number of marketers join together and share a prize budget in order to test the use of the sweepstakes. Co-op sweepstakes allow marketers to test the device in the same way that they would test other marketing tools. In addition, new computerized printing and mailing techniques will bring about cost efficiencies that will expand the market base for sweepstakes. Historically, we needed large customer bases for advertising because of the start-up costs involved in prize offers. Automation now removes much of the labor-intensive part of this business and will continue to make prize promotions more efficient for larger groups of businesspeople.

In the final analysis, however, the future of sweepstakes and other forms of prize promotion will depend not on technological wizardry and market research techniques, but, as always, on the application of the fertile imagination of the creative marketer.

CHAPTER NINE

Questions and Answers

During the authors' 20 years experience in designing and administering prize offers, some questions have come up repeatedly. Some are questions that every businessperson should have the answers to before even considering running a prize promotion; others reflect the complexity and subtleties of the prize promotion world. The following questions are most frequently asked.

QUESTION: Are prizes really awarded in prize promotions?

ANSWER: This important question we must address in order to gain the consumer's confidence. A businessperson conducting an offer may hear this question from customers, people within the organization, and the media—but it is most often asked by dubious consumers. If you use an outside independent judging organization, the simple statement, "We have retained an outside firm to handle this program," helps assure consumers that the prize promotion complies with all regulatory laws and that the prizes will be awarded fairly. Emphasizing the industry's careful regulation by federal, state, and local agencies, all branches of government, and Better Business Bureaus instills confidence that no sponsor would risk the tremendous legal problems and bad publicity that would result from noncompliance. Furthermore, the sponsor's committment to comply with state bonding requirements helps assure consumers that the offer is conducted fairly.

QUESTION: How can companies afford to offer multimillion-dollar prizes?

ANSWER: The prizes are simply another marketing cost. A company conducting a prize promotion is choosing one technique from among a multitude of marketing methods. For example, a company that has a $50 million advertising budget may decide to spend its available funds on this valuable method of advertising, while other companies spend their marketing funds on couponing, displays, or packaging. In most cases, the multi-million-dollar cost is a retail figure—the actual cost to the marketer is considerably less.

QUESTION: Within an organization, who has responsibility for prize promotion?

ANSWER: This depends mainly on the type of organization using prize promotion and how frequently they choose this marketing technique. For example, in a typical brand management system, brand managers report to divisional brand managers who report to the marketing director who, in turn, may report to the company's president.

A brand manager looks at prize promotion experts as one of the multitude of external sources that he or she regularly calls on. These may include the fulfillment house for premiums, a display house, or a public relations firm. In some companies where sweepstakes are an integral part of the business, these external services may include a direct marketing firm that uses sweepstakes as a part of its direct mail packages. There may even be a prize promotion manager within a company whose sole function is coordinating offers. This person's job would include interfacing with consumers, regulatory agencies, outside judging firms, creative and traffic people.

QUESTION: Where do prize promotions fit within the whole marketing mix?

ANSWER: There are a variety of promotional tools open to a marketer, including sampling, couponing, trade allowances, price-offs, premiums of all types such as in packs, on packs, near packs, and bonus packs, self-liquidators, refund offers, continuity premiums, and, of course, prize promotions. And there can be a staggering number of possible combinations. For example, we know that prize promotions can be conducted on their own, but frequently they are part of sampling or couponing programs to help increase the involvement in these offers. At present, many prize offers contain a guaranteed award that is nothing more than a premium. Essentially, consumers can enter with an actual proof of purchase or by sending in a 3 × 5 card; however, in the case of the proof of purchase, the consumer will receive a guaranteed award. That guaranteed award is, in fact, the premium. It might have a cost of handling or a liquidating price, or may simply be free in the mail.

QUESTION: What percentage of entries are accompanied by actual proofs of purchase?

ANSWER: This varies with the type of prize promotion. Obviously, where contests of skill are concerned and a proof of purchase is required, 100 percent of the entries will have proof of purchase. But remember, historically contests generate a low number of entries. In sweepstakes, however, the average number of entries with proof of purchase is 50 percent. A soft drink company may receive actual proofs of purchase with 80 percent of the entries in their promotion, while a car wax company may receive on 4 percent. The operative issues are the availability of the item, the price of the item, and the way the prize promotion is advertised. If the promotion is featured in news bulletins that go to regular contest entrants, these people will enter with the proof of purchase alternative. However, you need not be overly concerned with numbers of proofs of purchase unless, of course, this is a specific objective of the prize promotion.

QUESTION: How many entries does it take to have a successful sweepstakes?

ANSWER: The number of entries is seldom the criteria by which the success of an offer is measured. Even millions of entries can result in little marketing benefit if they are essentially multiple entries from readers of a contest news bulletin. Yet only 10,000 entries in a trade promotion can be an outstanding success if it achieved the desired result. In fact, one of the most successful offers we conducted received less than 100 entries. It was a display contest for which the trade was asked to put up a point-of-purchase display and take a photograph of it. Actual in-field research showed that many displays were built, but few people in the trade actually got around to consummating the offer by photographing the display and sending the photo in. Nonetheless, the objective was met with a very small dollar outlay. All too often, marketers and businesspeople look at numbers of entries to determine the success of their offer. But there is frequently little to be learned from such figures.

QUESTION: How often do winners of sweepstakes actually buy the product?

ANSWER: As a practical matter, businesspeople shouldn't be concerned about whether the winners buy their product. The goal of a sweepstakes is communication with the tens of thousands, hundreds of thousands, or millions of recipients of the offer. The one individual who happens to win a prize is of little significance in terms of the offer's marketing effect. As a matter of fact, statistics show that the winner is usually a nonbuyer. This is because many more entries are received without proof of purchase—especially in a direct mail sweepstakes. Sophisticated marketers are never concerned with the actual winner; they are concerned with the effectiveness of the offer.

QUESTION: In direct mail sweepstakes, the yes/no requirement means people can enter without purchasing. What percentage of people say yes and what percentage say no?

ANSWER: Again, this number should be of little concern to the marketer. Sometimes you will get as many as eight no's to every yes, while at other times you will get one to one. A number of factors, including the mailing list used and whether postage is prepaid, determines the yes/no ratio. Again, however, the key operating issue is whether there were more purchases made with a mailing that included a sweepstakes overlay than with a mailing to a similar size list without a sweepstakes overlay. When we add the additional cost of the sweepstakes prizes and administration, the question is simply: At what cost are we buying orders with a sweepstakes, and at what cost are we buying them without a sweepstakes? Thus, it is easy to determine whether a sweepstakes is cost-effective or not.

QUESTION: Once you start using sweepstakes, especially in direct mail, aren't you always locked into using them?

ANSWER: You are only "locked in" to the use of a device that proves effective. For example, a direct mailer who never enclosed a business reply envelope suddenly found that the benefit of doing so outweighed the cost; therefore, he continued to include business reply envelopes. Because certain direct mailers and package goods companies frequently use sweepstakes, a businessperson might think they are "locked in" to always using the device. But the explanation is simply that they have found a device that accomplishes their objectives at an efficient price and, therefore, it makes sense to continue using that device for as long as it works.

QUESTION: You spend a good deal of time speaking about setting objectives. Why is this so essential?

ANSWER: This question really relates to all business. Obviously, you can't obtain the desired result until you determine what result you desire. However, even the most sophisticated businesspeople who have clear objectives for advertising will sometimes simply say, "Let's do a sweepstakes." Yet, without specific objectives, we can't determine if the offer was successful. If the objective is clear, concise, specific, and realistic (i.e., "Let's increase coupon redemption 20 percent by using a sweepstakes overlay"), we can decide whether to continue using sweepstakes simply by asking, "Did we meet our objective?"

QUESTION: How important is the magnitude of the prize structure in a prize promotion, and what are the largest prize structures that have ever been offered?

ANSWER: We deal with this question in depth in Chapter Six. It's not surprising that there is a tremendous interest in the size of the offer. Although most sweepstakes have budgets of under $20,000, large offers do attract remarkable attention. Ventura Associates has administered the two largest offers ever conducted—whether measured by the total dollars of all prizes in a promotion or by the value of a single prize. Currently, the largest single dollar prize is Ventura's American Family Publishers' $10 million Grand Prize. The offer with the largest total prize budget was the TWA on-plane game offer. This offer, with more than 10,000 winners, was a trip to anywhere TWA flew. A trip to the farthest destination had a value in excess of $4,000. Therefore, the total value of the prizes exceeded $40 million.

QUESTION: Are there some destinations that are preferred by consumers? I notice that travel programs frequently feature such exotic destinations as Hong Kong or Paris, yet our own research shows that customers are not especially interested in these locations.

ANSWER: Your research is quite correct. Perhaps the most startling example is an offer we conducted in which 25 winners were offered a trip of their choice anywhere in the world. More than half chose destinations less than 1,000 miles from their homes. One woman in Tacoma wanted to see her sister in Spokane. The idea of traveling the long distance to Hong Kong, where people spoke another language, had little appeal to her. It is important to recognize that the appeal of the destination varies widely with the demographics of the winners. The destination is one more fine bead on prize selection. It is not enough to simply offer travel as a prize—you have to offer travel to a destination people are interested in.

QUESTION: What postpromotion opportunities exist in the promotion of the winners?

ANSWER: The notification of winners offers a tremendous business opportunity. All too often marketers believe that a prize promotion is over the day the sweepstakes closes. Yet major prize winners are big news—especially in small towns. Effective marketers request photographs and names of hometown newspapers from every winner. Distribution of these photographs along with a press release often results in great publicity for the marketer. Some towns have actually held parades in honor of major prize winners. And it's not only the million-dollar winners that make the news. Recently a woman who won over $100,000 received front-page coverage in a local newspaper and statewide publicity on radio and television.

Some specific types of prize promotions have unique, inherent public relations advantage. Prize promotions in which the winner is offered all the groceries they can pick up in five minutes have been conducted by a number of advertisers. Whenever the press is invited to the event, the result is major media coverage, occasionally nationally and almost always on the local television news. The vision of a local family dashing around a supermarket picking up groceries as fast as they can makes for a wonderful human interest story and is seen by the media as having special news potential.

QUESTION: I've often noticed in rules that the winners' names and likenesses will be used for publicity purposes. Does the information you give to the media have to be approved by the winner?

ANSWER: The answer is no. But since this is sometimes a touchy subject, it has to be dealt with in a professional and diplomatic manner. The rules and notification letters clearly state that names and likenesses of winners will be used in postpromotion publicity. The fact is that we don't need the winner's permission to do this, but we recognize the potential of ill-used publicity and are sensitive to consumers' concerns. We have found that by being conscientious we can usually quiet their fears.

QUESTION: How do you deal with requests for information about the program itself? Do you need to have the sponsor's approval?

ANSWER: Inquiries regarding the number of entries and the overall success of the program are not answered until we have the sponsor's consent.

QUESTION: Why do most people in your business refuse to answer questions over the phone and insist on inquiries in writing?

ANSWER: There are many reasons for our strict rule regarding telephone communication. As far as consumers are concerned, if we get a call requesting information about a prize offer, giving that information would give the caller an advantage over an entrant who does not call, which is obviously very unfair. In addition, people often misconstrue what they're told—they sometimes hear what they want to hear and not necessarily what is said. This is one of the main reasons for writing complete and precise rules. When we get a phone inquiry we tell the caller to take another look at the official rules. We respond to written inquiries only if the writer includes a self-addressed, stamped envelope. Can you imagine what it would cost us just for postage, to say nothing of labor and supplies? In addition, winner notification is also always done in writing. That way the prize is explained on paper, and there can be no misunderstanding about it.

QUESTION: The image of prize promotion still bothers my public relations department. Can you comment on this?

ANSWER: The image problem on prize offers exists more in the mind of marketers than the marketplace. As indicated in Chapter Four, appropriate prize offers can be created for *any* product—even the most upscale. Of greater importance is the actual experience in the marketplace. Marketers concerned about their image—American Express, Revlon, General Foods, Procter & Gamble, and General Motors, to name but a few—would not conduct these offers routinely if they believed that their offer had the potential to disturb their positive image in the community.

QUESTION: Can prize promotions work for upscale products?

ANSWER: Unquestionably. We know that the prize respondent has a certain psychographic profile. He wants to win a valuable prize. Marketers like Home Box Office, American Express, and *New York Magazine,* who sell to people in the top 20 percent income level, have found that prize promotions can solve specific promotion problems and can be created with any image desired.

QUESTION: I understand the importance of the independent judging organization to someone who has not run a sweepstakes before, but what expertise can such an organization bring to a firm that is an experienced user of prize promotions?

ANSWER: For even the most experienced user of prize promotions, the independent judging organization serves as a buffer between the consumer and the client. It provides a vital postpromotion service. Remember, with a sweepstakes you are talking to your valued customer. If any prospective customer is displeased with the outcome of an offer, there is a potential postpromotional problem. As the "outside" firm, we take the responsibility for dealing with such problems. The sponsor can diplomatically agree with their customer and then refer them to the third party—the independent judging organization. For any company that uses prize promotions, an independent judging organization provides the postpromotion services that are not available to them in-house, such as filing state and postpromotion bonds and fulfilling prizes. And, of course, it is the job of an independent judging organization to be constantly aware of changes in the law and other regulatory matters. Most users of prize promotions, especially companies that use them on a regular basis, rely on an outside organization to administer their offers. These include such diverse marketers as McDonald's and General Foods, both of whom have probably conducted hundreds of individual prize promotions.

QUESTION: What is the standard number of entries received in a sweepstakes?

ANSWER: Usually about 1 percent of the entry forms printed in newspapers, 2 percent of those printed in magazines, 5 percent of the entry forms distributed by direct mail, 6 percent of the entry forms distributed in freestanding inserts, and 5 percent of "take one" entry forms that are part of a display. (This number is based on the number of entries received from displays that have actually been used—obviously a vastly different number than the "take ones" that are printed and distributed.) Again, these figures may be useful for projecting returns but not for projecting success.

QUESTION: Do altruistic prizes ever work, such as the contribution of $10,000 in the name of the winner to his or her favorite charity?

ANSWER: There have been times when this device has been used to support a theme, such as a recent offer we conducted called, "Let Us Hear from You, America." The entrant was asked to write about what they would like to see in America and what changes they would like to make. The winner received $25,000 to spend on a trip and $10,000 to contribute to a local charity. Unfortunately, had the prize simply been a contribution to the local charity, few people would have entered. However, the client must balance altruistic desires with a desire to increase promotional results. We have never seen a specific prize promotion garner an impressive response if the winner were some third party. Even school programs, where the prize is won for an entire school, have never had the interest or success of traditional prize promotions.

QUESTION: With state lotteries giving prizes such as $20, $30, and $40 million, do you think it will be possible to maintain interest in prize promotions where the Grand Prize is considerably less?

ANSWER: If anything, state lotteries will generate new excitement because winning prizes will become more a part of consumers' everyday lives. Furthermore, in a state lottery, you must buy a ticket to win; in a sweepstakes you don't have to buy anything. In addition, in a state lottery, you have to go to a store, wait in line, and fill out a form. In a sweepstakes, entering is frequently as simple as checking a box and dropping the entry form in the mail. And finally, and perhaps most important, in many prize promotions the chance of winning is much greater than in a state lottery. The odds of winning in many state lotteries are astronomical.

QUESTION: Although you indicate that many sweepstakes have minimal budgets, have there been any award-winning, very successful sweepstakes that don't have huge budgets?

ANSWER: Many successful sweepstakes have minimal budgets. Again, we measure success by accomplishment of objectives. One example is the recent offer we conducted for a book called *Who Killed the Robins Family?* The idea behind this book and its related prize promotion is in the unusual nature of the book itself—it has no ending! Using the clues provided in the story, the reader had to determine who committed the murders, what the weapons were, and why the murders were committed. There was a single prize of $10,000. Although the book was well written, a major element of its success was the prize promotion. Many other mystery books produced at the same time had nowhere near the same success. Just how successful was this book? It was on the *New York Times* best-seller list for 26 weeks, resulting in major paperback sales, and it started an industry in its own right—the prize promotion book field—which has taken a variety of forms, including treasure hunts and trivia contests.

QUESTION: Looking at the popularity of lotteries today, couldn't the prize simply be game tickets in a state lottery with a chance to win the many millions of dollars they offer?

ANSWER: The Post Office prohibits transmitting or mailing lottery tickets. Therefore, there is no easy way to distribute tickets to the winner. In addition, we would have to be careful that the offer not be deemed deceptive. The winner would need to clearly understand that all they had won was a lottery ticket worth $1.

QUESTION: In general, is a sponsor of a prize offer liable for any income tax payments?

ANSWER: No. The recipient of the prize is liable for the tax payment.

APPENDIX A

Typical Administrative Fees and Services

BASIC SWEEPSTAKES SERVICES

The following are services that a full-service prize promotion firm should furnish in the planning and administration of a random draw sweepstakes.

The agency should:

1. Provide a continuing advisory service on any element of your sweepstakes that will contribute to its success. This includes conceptual development, layout and copy, prize structure, and program mechanics.
2. Give you the benefit of their experience in the practical application of federal, state and local lottery laws that could significantly affect your sweepstakes.
3. Write the official rules specifically for your promotion. Advise the participant of all unique features of your sweepstakes while offering maximum protection to the sponsor.
4. Review all copy, layout, and storyboards submitted in conjunction with your promotion for technical accuracy and compliance with the official rules.
5. Provide advice and counsel on the registration of sweepstakes in those states where required and provide surety bond forms for you to execute and return. Failure to comply in a timely fashion can result in substantial penalty.
6. Receive entries and determine winners in strict accordance with the official rules under procedures established for valid random drawings.
7. Verify winner compliance with entry requirements as established in the official rules.
8. Submit a standard certified list of winners (up to 1,500 names) after all clearances have been completed.
9. Guarantee that all information relating to this offer is held confidential and is secure against unauthorized use.
10. Guarantee the absolute noncollusion of the agency's employees with your company, its agents, and their employees.
11. Indemnify and hold you harmless from any loss, cost, or expense, excluding consequential damages, which you might incur or be subjected to by reason of any suit or

claim arising out of the agency's performance in handling your sweepstakes provided that you notify them in writing immediately upon your receipt of notice of any suit or claim set forth above and further provided that the agency be permitted to use attorneys of their own choice and that you cooperate fully with them and with their said attorneys. Indemnification is dependent upon your agreement to discontinue or revise the promotion as may be required. Implicit in this agreement is your timely completion of surety bonds or escrow accounts required as part of State filings.

You will indemnify the agency against all costs, expenses, and damages that may be incurred by the agency as a result of any claims or proceedings brought against the agency arising from any advertising or sales promotion activity undertaken without the agency's prior approval.

An estimated fee for all of the above services is: $5,000.00. Additional services which may be utilized are listed below.

ADDITIONAL SERVICES

The following is a partial list of additional services made available by many prize promotions firms. To assist you in establishing some preliminary budgets, estimated costs of the various services are listed. However, seldom are all the services used in any single promotion. Your account executive can assist you in identifying those you should consider.

A. Computer services:

• Programming standard 3-line	No charge
format each additional line at	$ 50.00
• Keypunching standard 3 lines	
for name and addresses	$ 100.00/M
Each additional line at	$ 10.00/M
• Duplicate name elimination	
standard 4 sorts	$ 20.00/M
Each additional sort at	$ 5.00/M

• Sorting to print—standard 3 sorts	$ 15.00/M
Each additional sort at	$ 5.00/M
• Printout	$ 150.00 (each)
• Pressure sensitive labels: standard label with names and addresses only	$ 50.00/M
• Custom-designed labels quoted separately	

B. For predetermined winner sweepstakes, including Lucky Number, Matching Sweepstakes, and games	$2,500.00

The agency should:

- Provide a plan for consecutively numbering or for preprinting winners.
- Indemnify that no more or less than the authorized number of winners is included in the overall circulation of the offer.
- Establish procedures whereby all major prizes are awarded in a second chance drawing.
- Provide a system for secretly identifying seeded major prizes.
- Verify winning claims.
- Establish seeding procedures on a valid random basis.
- Conduct second chance sweepstakes drawings to guarantee that all prizes will be awarded.

C. Trade sweepstakes in support of consumer sweepstakes	$2,500.00
D. Fulfillment services:	
Storage of materials	$ 30.00 per skid per month
Pick and pack	.10 per item
	at cost
E. Out of town travel from	$ 250.00 per person per day plus expenses

F.	Transparencies available immediately from Slide Library	$ 86.00 each
	Transparencies not used and returned within 48 hours	$ 5.00 each
G.	Post Office box rental: Per quarter or part thereof.	$ 130.00 each
H.	Screening of lucky numbers from prescreened sensitive digits	$ 30.00/M
I.	Custom books:	
	Original manuscript from	$2,000.00
	Typesetting per page	$ 12.00
J.	Personalized affidavit clearance letters and Personalized congratulatory letters	$ 9.50
	White mail	$ 5.00
K.	Processing of winners lists in excess of 1,500 names on computerized pressure-sensitive labels	$150.00/thousand
L.	Fulfilling requests (a request is a stamped, self-addressed envelope)	$ .14 each
M.	Furnish 1099 forms on all prizes we fulfill costing $600.00 or more	$ 18.50 each
N.	Legal opinion letter from outside counsel experienced in lottery law at federal, state, and local levels	$ 300.00–950.00
O.	State sweepstakes filings	$ 450.00
P.	Personal interview clearances	$ 300.00 (est.)
Q.	Prize procurement and fulfillment	Quoted separately
R.	Review of follow-up direct mail packages	Quoted separately
S.	All long-distance calls, messengers, postage, and overnight packages will be charged at cost.	
T.	Envelope opening	$ 35.00/M
	Extracting	.01 per item
U.	Art services:	
	Complete point-of-sale kits	

Sales brochures
Deal sheets
Take-one's
Riser cards

V. Print and Production
Take one's
Four-color brochure
Complete point-of-sale kit that includes our unique (patent pending) drop-off entry device, window and door banners, and take-one pad.

Price for all the above art, print, design, and production services cannot be quoted until specifications have been determined.

APPENDIX B

State of New York Department of State: Registration Statement Games of Chance in Connection with Sale of Commodities

STATE OF NEW YORK DEPARTMENT OF STATE

REGISTRATION STATEMENT
GAMES OF CHANCE IN CONNECTION
WITH SALE OF COMMODITIES

FORM G110-220 (8/78)

OFFICE USE ONLY

READ REVERSE CAREFULLY BEFORE FILING THIS STATEMENT

1. NAME AND ADDRESS OF PERSON, FIRM OR CORPORATION proposing to engage in game, contest or promotion:

2. Geographic area in New York State covered by promotion:
(List by county, if not state wide)

3. Description of game, contest or promotion:
(Not necessary if provided by your Rules and Regulations)

4. Time Period covered by contest:

Beginning

Ending

5. Minimum number of participating objects to be made available in New York State:

6. Minimum number of prize-winning objects included in plan in New York State:

7. Proportionate opportunity of winning prizes:

Level of Prize	Proportionate Opportunity

8. Minimum value of prizes to be made available in New York State:

9. Form Submitted by:

Name ______________________ Relationship to Firm ______________________

Address ______________________ Date ______________________

Signature ______________________

FILING INSTRUCTIONS

lease submit this completed statement to the **MISCELLANEOUS RECORDS UNIT, N.Y. DEPT. OF STATE, 162 WASHINGTON AVE., ALBANY, IEW YORK 12231** with Filing Fee of $50. (Please make check payable to N. Y. Department of State.) Fee is non-refundable.

Attach.

- —Certificate of Deposit of prize monies in a trust account **or** Surety Bond for total prize amount.
- —Rules and Regulations pertaining to the promotion, advertising scheme or plan

APPENDIX C

State of Florida Statement with Reference to Conduct of a Game Promotion (Sweepstakes)

STATE OF FLORIDA
STATEMENT
WITH REFERENCE TO CONDUCT OF
A GAME PROMOTION (SWEEPSTAKES)

____
(NAME OF SPONSOR)

Pursuant to the provisions of Section 849.094, Florida Statutes, the sponsor proposes to engage in a sweepstakes contest, offering the opportunity to receive prizes as determined by chance, and files the following statement:

1. Name of person, firm or corporation (sponsor of promotion)___

____

2. Address: ______________________________
(street) (city or town) (state) (zip)

3. Minimum number of participating objects (for example, entry blanks, tickets, etc.) to be made available: ______________

____

4. Number of prizes included in promotion or advertising scheme or plan: ______________________________

____

5. Proportionate opportunity of winning prizes: ______________

____

6. Minimum value of prizes to be made available: ______________

____

7. Rules and regulations: (Please attach) ______________

8. Time period covered: Beginning ______________

Ending ______________

9. Geographic Area Covered: ______________

Dated: ______________

____
(Name of Individual completing this form)

____
(Company, e.g., Agency handling promotion for Sponsor)

____
(Address)

Relationship to Sponsor: ______________

APPENDIX D

State of Rhode Island and Providence Plantations: Statement with Reference to Conduct of Games of Chance

Filing Fee: $100.00

STATE OF RHODE ISLAND AND PROVIDENCE PLANTATIONS

STATEMENT
WITH REFERENCE TO CONDUCT OF
GAMES OF CHANCE
BY

____
(Name of Promoter)

Pursuant to the provisions of Section 11-50-1 of the General Laws, as enacted by Chapter 199 of the Public Laws, 1972.

The undersigned proposes to engage in a game, contest or other promotion or advertising scheme or plan, offering the opportunity to receive gifts, prizes or gratuities, as determined by chance, to the value of prizes in excess of $500.00, and files the following statement.

1. Name of person, firm or corporation: ______________________________

2. Address: ______________________________
   (street) (city or town) (state)

3. Minimum number of participating objects to be made available: ______________________________

4. Minimum number of prize winning objects included in promotion or advertising scheme or plan: ______________________________

5. Proportionate opportunity of winning prizes: ______________________________

6. Minimum value of prizes to be made available: ______________________________

7. Rules and regulations pertaining to promotion or advertising scheme or plan, including the period of time and geographic area to be covered by the contest:

Dated: ______________, 19 ______

____
(Name)

By ______________________________
(Member of firm or officer of corporation)

Filed with Secretary of State ______________________________

FORM 300A 2½M 1-79

APPENDIX E

Games of Chance Surety Bond

Bond ________________

GAMES OF CHANCE SURETY BOND

KNOW ALL MEN BY THESE PRESENTS, THAT ______________________________
______________________________, a corporation duly organized and existing under the laws of the State of ______________________________ having its offices and principal place of business at ______________________________
(hereinafter called the "Principal"), and ______________________________
a corporate surety authorized to transact business in the States of Florida, and New York, as Surety, are held and firmly bound unto the Office of the Attorney General of the State of Florida and the People of the State of New York (hereinafter called the Obligee(s)) in the sum of ______________________________
______________________________ ($______________________________)
as hereinafter provided and as provided in 849,094 of Florida Statutes and Section 369e of the General Business Law of the State of New York, to which payment well and truly to be made and done, the said Principal binds itself, its successors and assigns, and the said Surety binds itself, jointly and severally, firmly by these presents.

THE CONDITION OF THIS OBLIGATION IS SUCH THAT:

WHEREAS, said Principal has filed with the Attorney General of the State of Florida and the Secretary of the State of New York to engage in a game, contest or other promotion or advertising scheme or plan pursuant to the provision of Section 849,094, Florida Statutes, and Section 369e of the General Business Law of the State of New York.

NOW, THEREFORE, if the said Principal shall well and truly perform and fulfill all of its undertakings and obligations, offered in such game, contest or other promotion or advertising scheme or plan as provided in 849,094 of Florida Statutes and Section 369e of the General Business Law of the State of New York, then this obligation shall be null and void, otherwise it shall remain in full force or effect.

PROVIDED HOWEVER, that Principal and Surety shall not be liable to all Obligees in the aggregate in excess of the penal sum of the bond.

IN WITNESS WHEREOF, the said ______________________________ has caused this instrument to be signed by its ______________________________ and its corporate seal to be hereunto affixed this ______________ day of ________________ 19______, and the said ______________________________ has caused this instrument to be signed by its ______________________________ and its corporate seal to be hereunto affixed this ________________ day of ____________________, 19______.

PRINCIPAL

BY:______________________________

INSURANCE COMPANY

BY:______________________________

APPENDIX F

Prize Winner Notification Letters

SALES PROMOTION

VENTURA ASSOCIATES, INC.

Congratulations! Your entry was drawn as____________________
in the ____________________________ Sweepstakes.

Your prize is

Please expect delivery within 6 to 8 weeks. Your prize will be shipped to the above address unless you notify us in writing immediately.

On behalf of our client, we thank you for your participation in this sweepstakes and wish you continued good fortune.

Sincerely,

VENTURA ASSOCIATES, INC.

Dana Johnson
Sweepstakes Director

200 MADISON AVENUE NEW YORK, NEW YORK 10016 212-889-0707

SALES PROMOTION

VENTURA ASSOCIATES, INC.

Congratulations! Your entry was drawn as ___________________
in the __________________ Sweepstakes.

Your prize is _______________________________________.

In order to confirm your present address and ship your prize, please complete the information requested below, and return it in the enclosed self-addressed envelope within __ days of the above date. Please allow six to eight weeks for delivery.

On behalf of our client, we thank you for your participation in this sweepstakes and wish you continued good fortune.

Sincerely,

VENTURA ASSOCIATES, INC.

Dana Johnson
Sweepstakes Director

Job #______ Sweepstakes:

Winner's Name: ________________________________

Please ship to (Name): _____________________________________

Address (P.O. Box Not Acceptable): _________________________

City: __________________________ State: _____ Zip: ________

Day Telephone #: (   ) _____________________________

Evening Telephone #: (   ) _____________________________

200 MADISON AVENUE NEW YORK, NEW YORK 10016 212-889-0707

APPENDIX G

Prize Winner Notification Letter and Affidavit of Eligibility

SALES PROMOTION

VENTURA ASSOCIATES, INC.

Congratulations! Your entry was drawn as __________________
in the ________________________________ Sweepstakes.
Your prize is ___________________________.

In order to verify your eligibility, confirm your present address and award your prize, the attached affidavit must be completed, notarized, and returned within _____ days of the above date. A self-addressed envelope has been enclosed for your convenience. Please allow six to eight weeks for delivery.

On behalf of our client, we thank you for your participation in this sweepstakes and wish you continued good fortune.

Sincerely,

VENTURA ASSOCIATES, INC.

Dana Johnson
Sweepstakes Director

200 MADISON AVENUE NEW YORK, NEW YORK 10016 212-889-0707

SALES PROMOTION

VENTURA ASSOCIATES, INC.

CBP_____

AFFIDAVIT OF ELIGIBILITY AND COMPLIANCE WITH THE OFFICIAL RULES/RELEASE

/ /

STATE OF________________________, COUNTY OF____________________,

I,___________________being duly sworn, depose and say:

1. I give this Affidavit to Ventura Associates Inc. with the understanding that this Affidavit will determine whether I am entitled to receive a prize in the __________________________ ("Sweepstakes") sponsored by ______________ ("Sponsor").

2. I hereby state that I have complied fully with all of the official rules of the Sweepstakes restated below:

3. I hereby grant to Sponsor the right to use my name, picture, portrait or likeness and voice in any future promotional material connected with this or any other sweepstakes conducted by Sponsor. I further agree that such use can be made without my inspection or approval of the use or any copy used in connection with it. (Note: A photograph may be submitted herewith. Or, if you do not wish to include this release, you may cross out this paragraph and it will not affect your opportunity to win.)

I AM OF FULL AGE AND HAVE READ AND UNDERSTAND THIS AFFIDAVIT.

____
Winner Signature

(Continued on back page)

200 MADISON AVENUE NEW YORK, NEW YORK 10016 212-889-0707

IF WINNER IS A MINOR, PARENT OR GUARDIAN MUST SIGN BELOW.

I, BEING THE PARENT OR GUARDIAN OF THE WINNER, HEREBY CONSENT TO THE WINNER'S ACCEPTANCE OF THE PRIZE, CONSENT TO THE WINNER'S EXECUTION OF THE AFFIDAVIT, AND AGREE TO BE BOUND BY THE PROVISIONS OF THIS AFFIDAVIT.

____
Parent or Guardian Signature (SEAL)

Sworn to before me this

__________________ day of ___________ 1985

____
Notary Public

____
Name (please print)

____
Street Address (P.O. Box Not Acceptable)

____
City, State, Zip Code

____
Social Security Number

____
Date of Birth

____
Day Telephone Number

____
Evening Telephone Number

Shipping Address if different than stated above (P.O. Box Not Acceptable):

____

____

____

APPENDIX H

Prize Winner's Travel Information Form

Prize Winner's Travel Information Form

Promotion:

Trip Destination:

Number of Days:

Number of Companions Permitted:

(Please type or print clearly)

Your Name:________________________________

Address:________________________________

City:____________________ State:______________

Zip:____________________

Travel Companion(s) Name(s) and Age(s):

Desired Travel Dates:

Trip must be taken no later than

First Choice:______________________________

Second Choice:______________________________

Third Choice:______________________________

Closest Major Airport:__________________________

Seat Preference:________Smoking ________Non-Smoking

Please specify any dietary restrictions:__________________

____

#

Note: An itinerary will be forwarded as soon as possible. Tickets and documentation will follow approximately two weeks prior to departure.

INDEX

Q-R

S

T

U

V

W–Z